Remarkable Tech Talent

GW00778310

Remarkable Tech Talent

A technical leader's guide to recruiting the best people in your industry

PAUL TURNER

R^ethink

First published in Great Britain in 2021
by Rethink Press (www.rethinkpress.com)

© Copyright Paul Turner

Contents

Foreword

Leading people is both rewarding and challenging. Depending on the phase of your own business, it may be essential to keep your people happy during optimisation phases by giving them a purpose to still see meaning in the work they deliver. Downscaling means for an excellent leader to be the number one go-to person to discuss personal fears, concerns – but to provide bad messages about reorganisations and cost-cutting. Upscaling turns out to be one of the biggest energy drains. Identifying, attracting and keeping great people is one of the most joyful and intense leadership tasks.

If you're in an upscale phase (congratulations) and trying to hire outstanding people then you know about the importance of having an excellent hiring process. Talent is rare, time is valuable, and competition is around almost every corner, especially in a metropolitan area.

Setting up a flimsy hiring process, not sticking to your process and not measuring your throughput time will be seen by the applicants in the market – your brand reputation and ability to hire is at high risk.

A core success criterion in your hiring process is *people*. The recruiters you work with are the first contact with your company, your organisation, your culture, your brand. These people need to understand you to draw attention to potential candidates. They sell your open position to the applicant. If they're right, you have access to great people. If they're not or they don't understand what you are, what you do, what culture you represent, you will not be successful in growing your organisation. Only a trusted and good partnership with your recruiters turns out to be fruitful for both: the leader and the recruiter.

Any one of you will most likely have experience with recruiters – both good and bad. Most people are familiar with the cold calling emails, unwanted phone calls, never-asked-for profiles which appear in your emails, the outreaches on LinkedIn and other social networks. But what can you actually expect from a good working relationship? What are the values of a good recruitment agency? What motivates good recruiters? How can we, as leaders, enable them to really be supportive and deliver a good job?

Paul Turner's book *Remarkable Tech Talent* gives a glimpse behind the curtain of the rationales of an excellent external recruiter, how they work, what they value and what they expect as a basis to help you find your best team. These insights helped me to better understand the importance of using a professional recruitment agency – and the value it adds to the important process of hiring the best workforce for your business. Not many of us think about the processes involved in recruitment but these processes can prevent personnel headaches, head off disastrous appointments and determine the success of your company. Read about them, reflect on them and improve your own recruitment process in an instant. It's good to get the mirror in front of you and your practices.

Enough of my words. Read the book, enjoy it – as I did – and draw your own conclusions. Make recruitment a better experience for your applicants, yourself and your business.

Michael Maretzke,
Chief Technology Officer, Temedica

Introduction

I have always enjoyed helping people. My working life in the service industry started early as a paperboy. I'd often go to pick up local groceries in addition to the papers I was delivering for older people who could not get out to the shops. I left college with no real sense of direction other than a hunger to get into the world of full-time work. I started off working in real estate and then became a local neighbourhood police officer. While I got a real buzz knowing I was making a positive difference, I missed the things that really interested me – football, gadgets and technology. The dream of being a professional footballer was out so I found my home in technical recruitment. It was a role that ticked all the boxes: I was in a position of genuine personal interest where the work I carried out could transform organisations and the lives of people within them for the better.

I believe the key to a company's success is hiring – if you want to secure the right people for your business, working with a tech recruitment agency or inhouse recruiter is the best starting point to propel your hiring. However, just working with a recruiter or agency will not get you far without understanding what a detailed search and selection process looks like and what value a professional recruiter can bring to your business.

The digital revolution is well under way. Business owners, chief technology officers (CTOs), chief information officers and tech leads face an uphill battle in competing for an already limited workforce in technology. It's incredibly tough to attract and retain critical technical people for business, and this can lead to a lack of clarity on generating growth. A-players are at the foundation of any successful business, and remarkably efficient recruitment is the only way to find them. There often comes two points in any business's life cycle where recruitment support is of the utmost importance:

1. Having hired key talent from your internal network, you need to decide how to find and engage new star players.

2. Having an existing team in place, you quickly need more resources to keep up with the success or scale-up of your business.

While your competitors might be wasting time on trying to continue to grow organically, businesses that have an exceptional partnership with outstanding recruiters manage to secure all the excellent people in the market quickly and continue to grow without the fuss.

Being in recruitment for close to fifteen years, I have always wondered why there was such a divide between recruiters or recruitment agencies and businesses who use or choose not to use them. This was the inspiration behind *Remarkable Tech Talent* – to give an overview of what working with a 'good' recruiter can look like.

I understand the pain-point of recruitment and the time it can take from creating a job; opening to closing it off; and 'onboarding', or settling in, the person you need. Many team or business leaders fear the associated cost of recruitment, especially if the selected hire does not work out. I want to guide you on what goes into the search and selection behind the recruitment curtain; what helps to position you as an employer of choice; and how you can minimise the risk of things not working out, whether you choose to work with an external agency or not.

This book advises you in how to make the critical decisions that will help you secure and onboard the talent you seek, add more value to your business and make your recruitment process more engaging. By the time you have finished this book, you will:

- Be clear on how to select the right recruiter

- Understand what a good partnership looks like and how to get the best out of your recruiter

- Stop making common thinking and action mistakes when hiring

- Know how to streamline your process

- Acquire some unique ways to make your recruitment genuinely stand out

Remarkable Tech Talent will take you through my detailed TALENT methodology. Mapping out how your recruiter or internal team should piece together a distinct process will make your recruitment a comfortable and streamlined journey.

If you are an entrepreneur, business owner or tech leader whose focus is on hiring technical talent for your business and you want to streamline and make your recruitment world-class, this is the book to help you cut through the noise and do it effectively.

Why not check out how your current process stacks up with our free online scorecard to see how good your process really is https://digitech.scoreapp.com?

PART ONE
THE WORLD OF RECRUITMENT

ONE

Recruitment Setup

Having an overview of the typical steps in your recruitment process (and the time it takes) will help you understand how important it is. A clear outline of your process is vital to ensure you are doing everything possible to secure the talent you want and that you are not losing them because of a substandard process. Couple this with working with an agency and you will want to make sure that the recruiter fully understands things from your side. This chapter outlines the foundations of what a good setup should look like and how your recruitment partners should run alongside it.

Process architecture

To establish the architecture of what your recruitment process should look like, I want to take you out of your position as a hiring authority and put you in the shoes of the person who must go through the process: the candidate. It's important to understand that these are *people* going through your process, not robots. The feeling they get from this recruitment journey is just as important as the process itself. I want you to *think* and *feel* what you would like to go through in a recruitment process if you were sitting on the other side of the desk. Question every stage: is this necessary? What loses my interest? What's enjoyable about it? Take a look at your current process with these questions in mind.

No one likes to go through a drawn-out, over-complex process that gives no clear outline of what happens at each stage. Everyone involved should be informed to make sure they understand the process in detail. The duration of a process from start to finish should take no longer than four to five weeks – anything more and the candidate will simply lose interest. Let's break this down to see what it looks like over a standard two-stage process without using an agency.

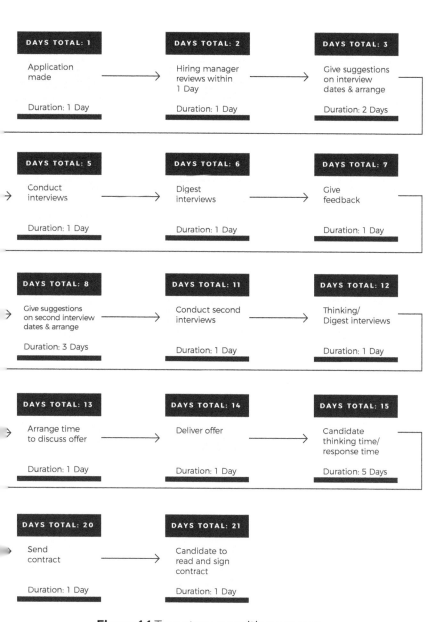

Figure 1.1 Two-stage recruiting process

The maximum number of working days for just a two-stage process totals twenty-one, and this is assuming that you are able to book interviews within the three-day period of availability. You can see how, if you take too long in your decision-making or you are not on point to schedule interviews quickly, you can soon make your process longer. If you have even more stages, imagine how long this process can get for a candidate. In my experience, good people in the market will not hang around much longer than a month when they are considering a new opportunity, so it's important to trim the fat and make sure your process is as streamlined as it can be.

There is a quote frequently attributed to Steve Jobs on the internet: 'The secret of my success is that we have gone to exceptional lengths to hire the best people in the world. I've participated in the hiring of maybe 5,000+ people in my life. So, I take it very seriously.'

A common problem often occurs in recruitment when hiring managers delegate different parts internally thinking that it will save time. At the end of the day, people buy people. Period. The same can be said about the candidate – they buy from their future boss. If the position you are recruiting for is in your department or your team then you are going to be the one who feels the pain of not having this position filled, not HR or a different department. If this hire has no impact on them the urgency to get something done is drastically reduced. This causes further delays to the process, which does nothing to improve your candidate's motivation for joining your company. Take responsibility for the process and be the driver behind it. If you have to involve other people or others need to be notified, cc them or use a collaborative Applicant Tracking System (ATS). (I will discuss the importance of a good ATS and one I personally recommend later.)

If you are working with a recruiter, lack of ownership of the recruiting process is often one of the biggest frustrations they have. Discussing the role, scheduling an interview or discussing feedback when it must go through another person not directly involved in the team is often a bottleneck that can be avoided. Recruiters appreciate direct contact and constant communication as it enables them to get the job done and ultimately help them to help you. A lot of hiring managers complain about having direct contact with their recruiter as they feel it wastes time. Trust me – if you employ a recruiter and then make them work through someone else with less information than you, then you are setting them up to fail and it will ultimately be a bigger waste of time for you. Both positive or negative information is helpful – if it's positive they will get the next steps completed as soon as possible and if it's negative, they should learn from it, which will help them in their continued searches for you. If the constant communication is an issue, agree on a time that works for you. If they ignore this, sack them and find a recruiter who can do better.

Once you have set out your process, you should make it clear to the recruiter so they know exactly what happens at each stage and can inform the candidate on what to expect. This keeps everyone happy. If you want to go a step further and stand out, I recommend putting a graphic on your website that outlines what the process is, or creating a short video clip welcoming the candidate into your process and describing what the stages are (and maybe why you do them) so that anyone who applies has an overview of what is expected.

Types of agencies

When it comes to selecting a tech recruiting partner it's important to understand how they are set up and what their strengths and weaknesses are to see how much of an impact they can have on your recruitment. There are two main types of tech recruitment companies: generalists and specialists.

Generalist tech recruiters

Typically, these can be found in a small agency setup that will recruit candidates into anything across the entire IT spectrum – they are a 'one-stop shop' for all your open positions. You will often have one point of contact who is usually responsible for all the recruitment that you do with them, which is useful and can help keep everything under one umbrella. It does take a special type of recruiter to service you well in this arrangement though. To work in this way and to be successful, your recruiter, as a non-technical person, will have to understand various types of positions in your technical team. The best way to check their competence level in multiple areas is to ask for their success background and how many people they have placed in different types of positions for one client. If you have found a recruiter that is able to understand and grasp things quickly as well as being incredibly skilled at multi-tasking, then this can work well. During my time in recruitment, I can probably count on one hand the amount of people I've seen able to do this to a professionally high level – they are a rare breed.

Generalists can be good if you want them to focus on one or two different positions, but their capacity is often limited. If they work this way with you it's likely they will also support other clients in the same way. If they are supporting anywhere upwards of ten clients, then their ability to support you on all your open positions will be limited. The way to get the best out of them is first understand how many clients they are currently supporting. If the number is high, then you will want to highlight which roles are your highest priority positions so that they have a focus. It's also worth trying to get an idea of where you rank in their priority list so you can feel confident you will get a return.

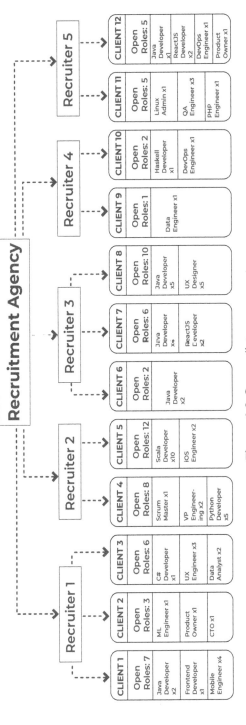

Figure 1.2 Generalist agency setup

The disadvantages of this setup are that your recruiter will not be knowledgeable of the specific technical area you are recruiting in, which can lead to a low level of results. They have a limited overview of the market and can only give you some useful information on a case-by-case basis. They are not really in touch with the market if it's a specific position such as a Java Developer, for example, and they will not be able to identify people quickly or understand who the movers and shakers in that area are. They are in reactive mode and will only be able to source talent after a much longer searching and understanding period. They may also have had no prior recruitment experience in that specific technology, which makes their job much harder as they will struggle knowing who to identify as a strong candidate. They often work across multiple locations which can leave them spread thinly. Generalists are good to use if you only recruit one or two positions per year.

Specialist tech recruiters

Specialist tech recruiters can usually be found in larger recruitment agencies in which the business has identified the specific technology or skill as a vertical specialism within the business. Here you are likely to find them working as a delivery unit to one customer with multiple points of contact for technology or geographies. If you work with a generalist recruiter, it is probably quite normal that you would work with more than one agency. The principle is the same here but instead you will only work with one company, which saves the headache of setting up terms with lots of different businesses and achieves the same coverage.

The advantages of using a specialist are that they will have a detailed knowledge of the specific area you are recruiting in so it will take less time to brief them on what you are looking for. They will be able to challenge your requirements to understand what is important. They will have a strong idea of what makes the position attractive to the target market and should be able to pick out and judge why someone is a good fit for your position as opposed to inundating you with CVs and hoping some of them will suit (which more commonly happens with generalist recruiters). An agency with a specialist setup will be able to cope with a high demand of positions as they will have a person dedicated to each work area. They will have a good overview of the market and knowledge of who is available, or if something comes up, will know who will be interested so that they can reach out to them straight away. If they are committed to a technology specialism, they might even have learnt the basics, which makes them even more valuable when pre-screening candidates for the position, giving you a higher win ratio of suitable people.

The disadvantage of this setup is that if there is a specific technical area that is not covered in one of the agency's specialisms, then they will not be able to support you as well as you need and you may need to find another recruiter or agency that will. It is worthwhile checking how the business is broken down into specialisms to see whether they cover the main areas you are looking to recruit for in your tech team. A quick overview of their website should be enough to give you an idea. Sometimes with this setup you can have too many points of contact in one business and if their internal communication is not good you can get multiple calls. The best solution is to ask for an account manager to handle all the communication with you or to schedule specific times when they are able to call you.

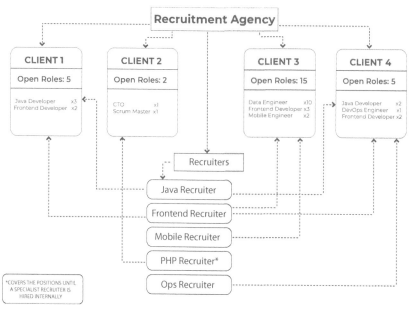

Figure 1.3 Specialist setup

Overall, there are pros and cons for both setups – which option you choose depends on your situation and how much recruitment you are looking to do. If you are a small company with a low number of hires, a generalist recruiter or agency will most likely be able to support your needs. You still want to ensure you are hiring someone who is competent enough to support you, so when selecting an agency, it is best to ask for references or success stories. If you are in a hyper-growth stage or a larger business, then a specialist setup will suit you well. Make sure that all the areas you recruit in are covered by their specialisms or you can end up using too many agencies.

Hybrid recruiters

Some agencies apply a hybrid solution which works well as it helps clients to benefit from both a specialist approach and a generalist pool. My company has adopted such an approach by breaking recruiters into two main areas. The first are the specialists who really dive deep into a particular technology. They are experts and can support clients in the specific areas they are recruiting in. If we do not have a recruiter for a particular technological area, then we use our second area – the generalist pool. This is another group of talented recruiters with a special ability to understand things quickly and multi-task. A hybrid method enables clients to feel confident they can depend exclusively on an agency to handle all areas of their tech recruitment to a high standard.

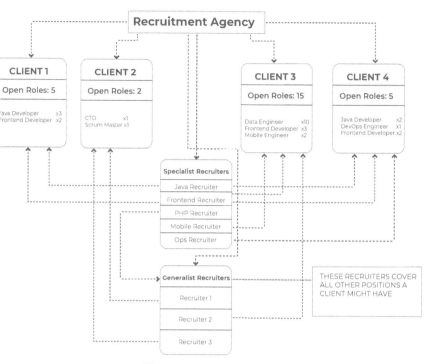

Figure 1.4 Hybrid setup

Selecting an Applicant Tracking System (ATS)

If you are working with an agency or not, a good collaborative ATS is vital to the success of hiring. It will help you track your candidates and manage the interview process accordingly. Beware, some ATS aren't great and act more as an internal database. There is often more than one person involved with the recruitment process so it's important to make sure you have a system that connects everyone in real time so that they know what's going on, preventing any delay in the recruiting process.

The hiring process using an ATS without a recruiter

Firstly, let's look at the hiring process using an ATS without using a recruiter. Here is a typical overview of a mid-sized but fast-growing tech business: a company has forty open positions within eleven different roles. They are using an ATS system, but with a lot of communication going through various channels such as email, software such as Slack and the ATS built-in messaging tool. The leading is done by the CEO alone. The result? Everybody is working on everything, there is no prioritisation on positions, and the company's brand reputation from applicants is getting badly damaged due to some candidates sitting in the ATS system for forty to fifty days without anybody noticing or giving any feedback.

To get the hiring process on track with an ATS there are some key things to do from the outset to avoid work piling up and getting out of control like this. These include:

- Appoint a team lead: The CEO or CTO can still lead but assign the hiring manager or team lead to take control and responsibility of the processes for each role falling within their team.

- Prioritise the positions.

- Explain the importance of the company's brand reputation to the hiring managers and have a Service Line Agreement (SLA) to answer applicants on time.

- Communicate clearly who has to do what and when.

- Keep all the communication in one place (this is where an excellent built-in messenger on ATS will come in handy).

- Organise bi-weekly check-ins from the leader to oversee the processes (you could also consider HR taking over this part).

By doing these simple fixes, you can start to get the process under control and improve the initial impression of your company's brand within your recruitment process. With an SLA to respond to candidates on time, be aware that reacting too fast can cause issues with some applicants feeling they have not been appropriately considered. I'd suggest finding a middle ground between three to five working days. Once you have optimised this process, you can then start setting out goals and objectives to get a certain number of positions closed per week or month.

The hiring process using an ATS with a recruiter

There can be a mindset when it comes to recruitment that businesses working with an agency should only discuss their real thoughts of a candidate internally.

This gives the recruiter a limited view of what the client actually thinks, or worse, no feedback at all. Think about that for a second: why would you go to the trouble to hire a recruiter to do a job then not bother to give them any feedback on the people they introduce? That benefits no one. Often the problem businesses have is that they don't have the time to duplicate their internal feedback, so the recruiter is usually the last to know and loses out with a filtered down or shortened answer. Having a tool that not only tracks the application process of a candidate but can also give an overview of all the communication about that candidate in real time solves that problem and makes sure that the feedback is as efficient as possible. Selecting an appropriate ATS will help to streamline your communication with a recruiter.

If you are still running Excel spreadsheets, shame on you! You need to change that – fast. Be sure to make a smart investment in your process with a tool that is efficient and fulfils all the tasks you need. There are a number of different ATS platforms on the market for your company to choose from to fit your specific needs. 'Workable' is the platform I recommend because it works seamlessly from start to finish. It enables a clear overview, easy communication, you can talk in real time and information is visible to all parties – including your recruitment partner.

Be clear on who's managing the ATS system and who's dealing with what in the overall recruitment process. If you have hired a recruiter, treat them like an employee or extension of your business. They are experienced in managing the ATS, which can be a headache to use and hard to upload profiles to if you're not familiar with it. So be sure to provide your recruiter with all the details. Good communication will avoid the annoying calls from your recruiter about status or latest updates and allow them to manage the ATS and solve a lot of logistical issues along the way.

While ensuring that most things are transparent and shared is good practice, this does come with a few issues. I totally appreciate that as a hiring manager you will not want sensitive information such as salary expectations shared. This is especially important if you have an employee of the same level who is involved with the hiring process and potentially able to see that information. Ensure you find an ATS with a function where you can choose what is visible as the administrator. If you don't, make it clear to your recruiter not to discuss or highlight salary unless otherwise requested.

I would avoid using platforms that do not offer open communication or visibility with the recruiter. Ultimately the recruiter will get frustrated using it and will revert back to sending you candidates via email. This causes more work as you need to add the candidates manually and receive status update calls. It can also deter the recruiter from wanting to work with you or even make your business the last company on their list to recruit for because of unnecessary admin.

I'm often surprised at how many tech businesses still don't have an internal ATS to help them co-ordinate their process. As a business leader, it's important to make sure you have a helicopter view to ensure that your process is as good as it can be – if a certain number of people are falling out of the process at a particular stage you need to know when, why and where. An ATS lets you address the problem to see if it's something you or the recruiter can analyse and change for the better. If you choose one that's right for your business, it will speed up the recruitment process overall.

Budgets/fees

When you are working with a recruiter, you need to understand what the typical pricing model of an agency looks like so you know how much it will impact the budget you have for the recruitment process. There are quite a few different pricing models that agencies use but this section will explain the basics so you can understand your options.

The fees are an interesting area to consider from both sides. Obviously as a business you do not want to be overpaying but going with an agency with the lowest fee is not always the wisest choice either. As a business owner myself, I have occasionally fallen into the trap of just going for the lowest price and usually ended up getting what I paid for – which wasn't good at all. A great quote, often attributed to Benjamin Franklin, is:

'The bitterness of poor quality remains long after the sweetness of low price is forgotten.'

You also have to consider that agencies often have more than just you as their client. If you drive too much of hard bargain and push the percentage or fee too low, it will make the recruiter feel less incentivised to want to work for you compared to other clients. If you have two clients both looking for similar profiles – one paying you 15% and the other 25% – which one would you feel more inclined to introduce your best candidates to?

Typically, a permanent recruitment agency will charge a percentage of the hired candidate's salary for the first year as the fee for the service, or what's known as a 'finder's fee'. Most agencies apply the success-based model, often referred to as 'no success, no fee'. This means that when you are selecting a recruitment agency to work with, you normally get a chance to try them before you buy with little risk. This is a great way to see if the agency is any good. They will only get a fee one of two ways: once a candidate you like signs the contract to work with you, or on the first day of employment with you. The percentages range in different markets or geographies but in the IT area the fee usually ranges from 20–30%.

The best recruiters I know generally understand their worth and will tell you if the percentage you are offering is too low for them. It's basic economics. Ultimately, you are the judge of what adds more value to your business and what is worthy of the investment. This is often why a 'success only' fee is a good way to start the business relationship together, allowing you to see first-hand if your recruiter of choice is suitable for finding the people who can take your business forward in the direction you want and so warrant the fee.

When discussing fees, it's often overlooked but it's worth asking what you actually get in return for the overall end payment. Most recruiters will tell you the person/candidate is the result, which is a lazy answer. What you need to understand is the work that goes into finding this person. Get them to explain their processes and what they do to help you uncover the person you are looking for. The best recruiters will be able to clearly articulate their process and the value-add they bring to recruiting the best people for your business.

The other typical model in recruitment is the 'retained search'. The setup here is usually where you split the fee into two or three parts. The overall fee, again, is based on a percentage of the candidate's salary for the first year. If you agree to work together, the first part of the fee is usually paid upfront to 'retain' the services of the agency. The second part of the fee is on delivery of an agreed number of candidates shortlisted, and with payment made for the individual who commits to interview for the position where you have split the process into three parts. If you have split it into two parts, the remainder (or last part of the fee) is paid once a candidate signs the contract or when the candidate starts work.

The advantage of the retained model for you is that the agency will probably be able to allocate more time and resources to getting the position filled. It also allows your open position to be a higher priority for the recruiter and puts the recruiter under a bit of pressure to ensure they fill the position. If it's a critical hire and you decide to work on a success basis with the recruiter, you will not have any way of knowing if the agency is working on it or if it's a priority to them. This could force you to lose valuable time by not having this commitment upfront.

If it's a priority position for you to fill I highly recommend using the retained model as it is most likely to bring you results. The danger is that you could be paying a fee with no guarantee that the position will definitely be filled, so only do this type of search once you have had some success with the recruiter and feel confident enough that they will deliver or if you have had a strong recommendation from someone you trust that they can do this job well.

TWO

Common Mistakes

Being in technical recruitment for over fifteen years I have seen what works and what doesn't. After speaking with thousands of business and tech leaders, I noticed there were eight common underlying thinking and action mistakes when it comes to tech recruitment. This chapter addresses how these mistakes can be avoided and includes advice to help you to focus on hiring more A-players without fuss.

Mistake 1: People apply directly

Overview: Today's tech job landscape is a competitive one – every company wants the next best engineer and is jostling for position as 'an awesome place to work'. If you are not vocal about your business or reaching out to people directly, you will not attract A-players or create a buzz about your business. If you are not doing this, then fewer people will be aware of your business until the applications ultimately grind to a halt.

Thinking mistake: A lot of business leaders have a biased perception of their business. They feel that their company is an 'amazing place to work' and people should just apply for positions directly. The truth is, unless you are one of the well-known brands in tech such as Google, Facebook or Amazon, you just won't get the same level of applications and you have to work a hell of a lot harder to get noticed.

Action mistake: As a result, business owners typically follow the traditional route by having a jazzy careers page on their website along with the open job positions, or they place an advert and don't do anything else. They expect the applications of well-suited, A-player candidates to start flooding in and they may get the odd applicant if they are lucky, but the reality is, they just won't.

Why it's a mistake: Many leaders think they don't need to actively work on their brand in the recruitment market and only post jobs on their website or popular job boards. Their business then misses out on opportunities to secure the best people who are passive in the market, which makes their recruitment harder as they struggle going through hundreds of irrelevant applications or ones that are just not at the level they were expecting.

Solution

Your business is probably a great place to work but no one knows that unless your business is already well known and there are plenty of ways to do this. Here are some ideas:

- Ask your existing employees to write a short review of what it's like to work there. People often use platforms like Glassdoor to get a feeling of a business before applying. Reviews on Glassdoor are anonymous so employees can confidently give honest feedback. If your business is as great as you think it is, these will help promote it. If some of the comments are below what you expect, it can also provide you with the opportunity to address areas in the business that may need improvement.

- Get your content out there. Good people don't always look for new jobs – they like to read, watch, listen and get a feeling of your business through multiple channels before even considering applying. Share videos of the workplace, share your ideas and team events and publish articles on LinkedIn, Instagram, Facebook, etc. This helps create a buzz about your business and allows people to connect with you.

- Hold 'meet-ups': Use your office space to get involved in the community. Let people visit and see what you are about. This gives people a first-hand look at your environment. Without trying to sell jobs to them, you are subconsciously giving them the opportunity to enquire and become interested.

- Hire a professional recruiter. This is an obvious choice considering my background in recruitment, but as a business owner myself the amount of time (and ultimately money) you can save with someone who knows what they are doing is invaluable. Once you have a recruiter or an agency that knows the score, they can help promote your brand and business. They'll also bring some unreachable or passive talent to the table to really uncover a handful of A-player candidates.

These small changes can really make a big difference in helping you attract more people to the business and to get your name out there in the tech community.

Mistake 2: HR does all the recruitment

Overview: A lot of people associate recruitment with HR or think they perform the same function. They don't. If you are hiring for a tech position, unless that person ends up working in HR, the candidate will have little interest in speaking with them. A tech candidate will want to talk to the tech leader to understand the position, who they will be working with, and what the challenges will be. HR will not be able to answer in detail, which can lead to the candidate losing interest.

Thinking mistake: As HR is often involved with the process, business leaders think they can unload all the work involved with recruitment onto the HR department. Recruitment is only a small percentage of what HR actually do and if the position does not directly impact their department, they will not feel the pain as much as the hiring leaders and their teams.

Action mistake: Business leaders dump all the core functions of recruitment onto HR. They ask them to take control of the entire process and only get involved in the process at the end.

Why it's a mistake: HR is an important part of the process, but they should not completely control it. People want to work for you, not HR. The connection between the hiring manager and the candidate needs to be strong from the first step in the process.

Solution

If the position is in your department and under your direct responsibility, get involved with the recruitment process from the beginning. Here are some ideas to assist:

- Make sure you are screening all the resumes that come in as it will stop you from losing a few gems that HR could miss by only looking for buzzwords.

- Working with an experienced recruiter/talent acquisition specialist who understands exactly what you are looking for can help to reduce 'screening time'.

- Ask HR to support you with scheduling if necessary, but don't lose control of the whole process.

- It's good practice to cc HR on everything you do so they know what's happening and can act when needed. Using an ATS like Workable for collaborative recruitment is helpful for this.

Mistake 3: I can do it all myself

Overview: At a glance, recruitment seems easy enough. Business leaders often see the whole process through rose-tinted glasses, but things can (and do) go wrong, and if there is more than one position open the process gets more complex.

Thinking mistake: When a leader has an open position it's easy to think, 'I can do this. I'll get some candidates in, interview them, make an offer to the best one, agree on the deal and then voila, done.'

Action mistake: Typically, these tech leaders end up writing the job specification, posting an advertisement, waiting for the applications to start coming in and then hope for the perfect match. Next, they review all the applications and need to call each one to pre-screen them. For most tech jobs they will ask the candidate to conduct a test, which they must spend time sourcing or creating themselves. If all this goes well, then they make an offer to the candidate directly and try to negotiate the deal. Once complete, they'll have to draw up the contract, send it out, and then stay in touch with the person until the start date as well as plan the onboarding.

Why it's a mistake: Recruitment is clearly a time-consuming piece of work – if you allocate all your time to recruitment you will have no time to complete other important tasks in the business. Recruitment should make up 10–20% of a tech or business leader's job. Another disadvantage of dealing directly with candidates is that you might miss concerns as they often feel awkward voicing them in case it will impact their chances of getting the job. If they have other options on the go, it's also likely they will not inform you. Being unaware of your competition can lessen your ability to negotiate effectively or close the deal.

Solution

Trying to do all the recruitment yourself can lead to burnout and make you lose enthusiasm for, and your personal touch towards, recruitment. Making the process a team effort will allow you sufficient time to focus on running other aspects of your team or business. Consider the following ideas:

- Recruiting is a team sport. If your process is internal, then you must pull on all the resources available to you.

- Partner with an amazing recruitment business or talent acquisition partner you can trust. If you don't know one, speak to your network – ask around for recommendations. If you are selecting a recruitment agency, do your research as it can be a bit of a minefield. A good indication is to look at the specific recruiter's references which should be visible on their LinkedIn profile or website.

Recruiters will tend to work a lot harder for you if they are working exclusively, as it's a better deal for them and they can feel confident they will not be wasting their time or having to compete with too many variables. Exclusivity doesn't cost you anything financially. Try exchanging exclusivity to get the price down, but not too low that the recruiter feels it's not worth it.

Mistake 4: Working with agencies is too expensive

Overview: Many people think that working with a recruitment agency is just too expensive. If you weigh up all the costs and time taken to do the search and selection of candidates though, you'll find it a worthwhile investment.

Thinking mistake: Thinking that the costs are too high causes many tech leaders to completely disregard the idea of seeing whether the benefits of working with an agency will be worth the investment. This often comes from either not knowing enough about the market or not knowing what the actual cost of recruiting someone is.

Action mistake: These tech leaders tend to become a closed book and will not entertain any conversations with recruiters or agencies, choosing to rather try and recruit directly.

Why it's a mistake: Consider this example of an annual salary of 100,000 EUR. Broken down monthly this is 8,333.33 EUR. With about twenty working days a month, this equals 416.66 EUR per day. Divide this into an average working day of eight hourly segments and you have 52 EUR per hour. How many hours a day do you spend on recruitment tasks? Writing job adverts, going through every CV received and managing the process as a whole takes up valuable time that could be better spent in other areas of the business.

Solution

How much is your time worth? I'm guessing a lot if you run a business or if you are responsible for a division or team. Take a helicopter view of this. Isn't that time worth investing where it's most valuable? The simple answer should be, *yes*!

- Team up with an agency or talent partner that is right for you. Remember, a lot of agencies work on a success basis. A big part of the time they save you is spent on the search and selection part of the process.

- Recruiters are skilled at head hunting and can reach candidates – including unreachable or passive talent – far quicker than you will be able to.

Speak to other business owners or tech leaders, do a Google search, visit recruitment websites and check out testimonials to find out who is doing an amazing job in what you are looking to recruit for. For every bad recruitment business out there, there are remarkable ones. It's your job to find the one that will give you the best return on your time investment.

Mistake 5: My job advert is enough

Overview: This is one of the biggest areas of recruitment that could do with a complete overhaul. Think about it – when considering a new job, how boring is it to read through a description that has no real identity?

Thinking mistake: Most tech leaders, or leaders in general, think this is usually the answer when recruiting people and feel a written advert will be enough to attract the right people to the position.

Action mistake: Writing the job description or advert should be the easy part of recruitment but when you get down to it, it can be quite difficult. Most descriptions usually follow a similar format. They give:

• An introduction to the business

• A few bullet points on the job's responsibilities

• A 'wish list' of skills the business is looking for

• Some benefits of the job or joining the business

The advert is then posted on the company's website or a couple of job boards and left to do its magic so the leaders can sit there and wait for the ideal candidates to apply. Or not, as the case may be.

Why it's a mistake: Job adverts are everywhere – and ultimately all the same. In reality, they can be pretty boring – there is often little to engage with and no way to show your enthusiasm for your line of business or your organisation. It's difficult to convey all the challenges you have in your open position. You cannot show what it's like to work there or the culture of what's cool about your business. Just releasing job adverts will not find you the A-players.

Solution

It's time to rethink the job advert. Take it out of the stone age. A-players don't spend time reading job ads – hell, they don't even look for new jobs. If you want the best people in your business you have to be proactive and add a human element to get people interested, or you have to try really hard to stand out. If you must have a job advert, here are some ideas to improve them:

- Most job ads have a 'wish list' – ie the skill or requirement section. This is the first part that often goes wrong. Be real with this – don't just fill it up for filling up's sake. Trim off the fat and state the facts. If you must have more detail, the best way to do this is to list the 'must have' skills followed by the 'nice to have' skills.

- Job ads do not have to be formal. Be creative and make it stand out. You could even get rid of the traditional ad altogether and replace it with a video. Make it more engaging and distribute it in places that your targets (including passive candidates) spend their time rather than on the standard, uninspiring job boards.

- For even better results, actively pinpoint the people you want and write targeted emails to them, *not spam* messages.

- This can be a great opportunity to involve the team. Ask them what they think is important for the role. If you have someone in a similar role, ask them to tell you what's cool about it. Get geeky, ask them what kind of things would attract them or pique their interest.

- Talk technology, highlight the actual technical challenges. Maybe start with the challenge you are working on right now and what's in the pipeline for the future. If it's written for engineers, then like most engineers I know, the more complex and challenging the problem is, the better.

- If your product or service has kudos in some way, talk about it and bring it to people's attention. Does your product reach millions of people? Good – tell people about it. Is your service unique? Great – explain how.

- Always try to write the ad in a way that looks at it from the candidate's perspective as well. I particularly like closing an ad thinking 'what's in it for them?' This is your chance to really show off all the great things you do for your employees and why people should get excited about applying to work for you and your organisation.

Once complete, don't be complacent – test it. Ask your recruiters what they think. Does it capture their attention too? Most recruiters should be able to analyse it well enough to give you the thumbs up. When speaking to candidates, ask for feedback about your ad and if it did the job well. If not, understand why and keep improving it.

Mistake 6: I have no time for recruitment

Overview: For most leaders, the running of a team or business is difficult and as your leadership responsibilities grow, it's easy for recruitment to become less of a priority in your daily schedule.

Thinking mistake: Business and team leaders mistakenly think that they have no time for recruitment and that their commitment to the process does not have to be consistent.

Action mistake: Thinking that you have no time for recruitment usually leads to failing to allocate time for it.

Why it's a mistake: Your business will not grow and scale to meet the demands of the business efficiently without addressing recruitment. People buy people. If you want the best business possible, you need the best people possible. Rest assured, even if you don't invest in recruitment, many of your competitors will and they will land people you want and leave you wondering why they are outperforming you.

Solution

If you take on a leadership role you should know that recruitment should always be part of your job. Even when you don't have a position open and you're not actively recruiting, you should always keep an open mind for potentials. Don't pass it on to someone else – if it's your team, build it into your daily or weekly routine. Allocate 10% of your time to it regardless of whether or not you are actively looking.

- Remember, A-player candidates are not always available when you are and vice versa, so keeping an open door means you are agile and able to react when someone good comes along. Maintaining regular contact with your talent partner or recruiter pays dividends. Ask them to keep an eye out or to continue searching for exceptional people. It pays to be picky when you are not active – inform your recruiter of the situation and explain you will only consider someone if they match the requirements exactly. This way you have peace of mind that you are not missing out on anyone.

- When you're not directly recruiting, use the time this frees up on ways to improve your process or promoting your personal or business brand via social media. This ensures that when it is time to recruit, more of the people you want will already be aware of your business. It may even prompt A-players to approach you directly when you're not actively looking or ask you to reach out to them when you are, saving you time and effort before a new recruitment drive. If you have a team member leaving, it can also help you react quickly to backfill their position.

Mistake 7: Multiple points of contact

Overview: This is directly linked to businesses working with a recruiter or agency and does not always apply if they are recruiting directly or have an internal recruiting team. During the recruitment process with a recruiter or agency, it's typical that a business will have more than one stakeholder who liaises with them.

Thinking mistake: When a business has a recruiter who is actively searching on its behalf, and there are multiple people involved in the process, the business leader assumes that the recruiter will consolidate all inhouse opinions to find the perfect candidate.

Action mistake: Many businesses have two or three people the recruiter needs to liaise with, for example, the hiring manager, HR, the CEO, PAs, and so on. While it's important to take account of all of these people's opinions in the decision-making process, it can often be confusing for the recruiter or agency as they can be faced with conflicting information.

Why it's a mistake: Having multiple contacts can cause a bottleneck, especially if one of those involved is away on holiday or sick leave, unreachable or just too busy to contribute.

Solution

Recruiting is a team sport, but you have to make sure everyone is on the same page with what you are looking for. You must have a clear decision-maker who is directly heading up the team to liaise with the recruiter.

- Whoever is in charge of the team and feels the most pain of not having the position filled should be the main point of contact with the recruiter to do the following:

  - Give the briefing on the position

  - Be the sole person to send CVs to

  - Make the decisions on whether or not to interview

  - Receive and give feedback

  - Discuss offers

- If there are other people who need to be informed, tell your recruiter who needs to see what information and ask them to cc all relevant parties with the information. Selecting anyone else in a different department to do this will most likely lead to a lack of information that can cause the recruiter to misunderstand exactly what you are looking for or what is happening. This problem often occurs when HR blocks recruiters from speaking to hiring managers. If your process is driven by HR, ensure all necessary information is shared with the recruiter. Involve the recruiter with all internal communication as it will help them help you. As discussed already, an ATS such as Workable keeps all the communication in one place and informs everyone who needs to be kept informed.

- The success of your business absolutely depends on the people in it and is why the collaboration of your team and being directly involved with the recruiter should be your utmost importance as a leader. A good product or service will always just be that – a product or service. Without the great people behind it, it will never be anything more. Remember, *people buy people*, so the earlier you can be in direct contact with the candidate, the better.

- If you are out of the office for a few days, you do not want to slow your recruitment process down or risk losing some of the good candidates you have already lined up so tell your recruiter about planned holidays or business trips well in advance. This way you can both work around the dates to make sure your schedules are clear or that you both know you need to close up an existing process around a certain time and not to start any new ones. The worst thing a candidate can hear part-way through the process is that 'the manager has gone on holiday for two weeks, so we have to put this on hold and pick this up when he/she is back'. What right-minded A-player candidate is going to wait around for that long? It certainly won't fill them with confidence that you are really interested in hiring them.

- If there is an ongoing requirement and you cannot afford to stop or pause the recruitment while you are absent, I suggest bringing in your second-in-command – someone who also feels the pain of not having this position filled. It should also be someone you trust to make a judgement call on your behalf and who has the authority to make the offer – it's pointless getting them to step in and then still have to wait for you to give the green light at the end of the process.

Mistake 8: Taking your time

Overview: When it comes to recruitment, business leaders (myself included) want the luxury of time to be able to compare as many people as possible for an open position and to get the opinion of as many people as possible from the existing team to feel confident they are making the best-informed decision.

Thinking mistake: Hiring managers who feel they have plenty of time when it comes to filling a position do not tend to think about their internal process as being part of the problem of securing candidates.

Action mistake: This can lead managers to activate a process with too many steps, allow too much time between interviews, and take too long to gather feedback from everybody involved. In turn, this delays the scheduling of interviews making them too far in advance.

Why it's a mistake: The best people do not hang around for jobs. Often, the businesses that manage to secure the people they want make it happen and do so quickly. If you leave it too long or your process is too drawn out, your candidates will lose interest. This lets your competitors swoop in and secure the people you want to hire right from under your nose.

Solution

To guard against this, you need to commit to making your recruitment process as streamlined as possible. Put yourself in a candidate's shoes: how does it feel when a company comes back to you quickly versus one who doesn't? Here are some ideas to assist with streamlining the process:

- If someone applies for the position, get back to them the same day or next working day. It's remarkable how much of a difference that can make.

- Reduce the number of people conducting the interview to only those needed to make a decision regarding the candidate. The fewer people involved, the more agile you will be.

- Book interviews within the next three working days. Stop organising them two weeks in advance. In reality, would an in-demand tech professional wait around for two weeks just to see you? Not many, if any, will.

- Give feedback within twenty-four hours. It's important not to rush decisions but get your notes down while it's fresh in your mind. Build in five minutes to debrief yourself after the interview, then come back to them the next day and add anything you think of after you have slept on it. Make your decision and inform the candidate right away.

- If moving forward, suggest the next steps, ideally proposing a date within the next few days. If it's a no, it's just as important to inform the candidate and provide reasons. Not getting any feedback or having to wait several days for feedback is frustrating and can damage your brand reputation. Remember, people are more likely to talk about bad experiences.

- Put a one-week time limit on a decision. In most cases, people make an immediate subconscious judgement whether they want to work for you or not, but it's important not to push them so hard that they feel forced into making a decision.

Once you have done everything you can to streamline things, you can feel confident that your process is as quick as it can be. When a candidate has your offer, the ball is then in their court. Setting a one-week time limit also puts your competitors in a difficult situation if they are not able to move as quickly as you. In most cases, the candidate will not want to lose your job offer and most likely have to cancel other applications that can't close in time, leaving you in pole position to secure them.

The biggest pitfall of all

Hands down, not being fast enough in your recruitment process is the most common mistake you can make. If you hear people say, 'Recruitment is tough,' or, 'There's a war for talent,' or, 'No one accepts our job offers,' then I can tell you that they are most likely excuses for a poor process that just takes too damn long.

I cannot stress this point enough. The speed with which you can go through your recruitment process and having it as streamlined as possible are the key ingredients to securing people you want.

It's well known in the industry that people's motivation levels drop the longer they wait to hear back from you. This is also a crucial point to consider when giving feedback or making an offer – timing it just right and making an offer at the point when motivation levels are at their highest is the best way to secure someone.

The graph below outlines the motivation levels of a candidate as they go through the recruitment process.

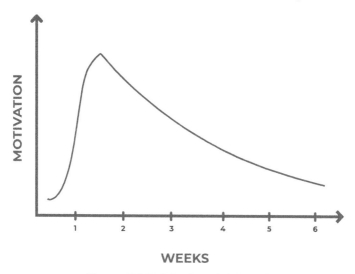

Figure 2.1 Point of peak interest

During week one and two, motivation is steadily climbing, usually during the interview stages. Once complete, the weeks following show how someone's motivation levels drop significantly.

I've recruited for many companies over the years. Time and time again we have introduced good candidates to clients and lost them in the process due to another business reacting faster and getting through their process more efficiently. I've had a case of sending a CV where the manager took two weeks to respond. By then, the candidate had four other processes in place, had received two job offers, and already accepted his next position. On and then off the market – just like that. The hiring manager was shocked, 'What? How can they be gone already; you only just sent the CV to me?'

Ultimately, A-player talent does not hang around. Companies that recognise this end up securing the people they want. Look at your own process – do you have too many steps? Do you respond quickly enough to applications? Do you need to wait for too many internal people to be available to meet this person? Do you take too long to give feedback?

With the shortage of tech talent available and the number of tech jobs out there increasing, this will only become harder. That's why beating your competition with a well-thought-out and streamlined process is the best way to secure people. If you can trim down the amount of time from application to offer you will be able to secure more of the tech talent you want. Anything from two to four weeks should be your benchmark for the whole process from start to finish.

PART TWO

RECRUITMENT STRUCTURE

THREE

Setting The Ground Rules

Having outlined some of the most common mistakes that are made in recruitment, I can concentrate on showing you what a world-class partnership with a recruitment agency can look like. One of the first things you want to make sure you have in place is good communication – this will enable effective collaboration.

Lines of communication

Before setting up a recruiter, you first want to set out some ground rules of what you expect from them and what you promise – this will show there is a strong commitment from both of you at the outset. Successful recruitment takes teamwork; clear expectations from the beginning facilitate the recruitment of the best top talent for your business.

Clear lines of communication are critical in establishing good working practices. Decide when is going to be a good time you can speak together. You might want to set out a weekly or bi-weekly schedule to speak every Friday at 10am for a maximum of fifteen to thirty minutes, for example. Or perhaps you can suggest having ten minutes any time between 5–6pm at the end of every day to discuss recruitment topics if needed. The key here is to try and establish a routine when you can both speak which will not interrupt the day too much.

TOP TIP

I advise discussing things over the phone rather than by email. You can get far more things done during a short five- to ten-minute phone call than you probably could over several time consuming emails back and forth.

Communication options, other than traditional phone calls, include Skype or Zoom calls – you can talk in real time without disrupting your day too much. WhatsApp is becoming increasing popular as it's also real time, and because it's on most people's smartphones it makes communication flow more quickly than on desktop. If you haven't considered trying this before I suggest you do to see how much it can speed things up. If scheduled phone calls are not an option as your day is too varied, having a good ATS in place will really help. Another option is instant messaging, but most likely your last option.

Ultimately, it's up to you establish the best methods of communication. However you decide to work, be transparent and inform the recruiter of the process you would like to follow – this helps to manage expectations all round. Take two minutes to draw up a short document with the process you would like and send it to them.

For example, you might want to say:

1. Send me all CVs via our ATS only. If you have a CV that's speculative, email it to me directly.

2. For feedback on CVs please call me on my mobile. I am free for these discussions during 4–5pm most days.

3. For scheduling interviews please use the ATS. I will give you open time slots there.

4. If there are any changes or other dates we need to look at, please ping me on Skype or WhatsApp so I can react quickly.

5. Interview feedback or offer negotiations are best over phone during times mentioned above. If that's not possible let's discuss it over Skype or WhatsApp.

6. For anything else please ping me first on Skype or WhatsApp and I will reply in due course.

Or if you want to be simple:

1. Please send me all CVs by email.

2. All communication thereafter is best for me over Skype (chat and instant messaging).

Secondly, it's good to set out some goals. If you have multiple requirements, it's best not to dump the whole load on the recruiter at once as this will leave them feeling overwhelmed or not knowing where to start. It's good to prioritise what you have open. Get the most urgent positions looked at first and explain to the recruiter why they are so urgent and when you need them filled by. A good tech recruitment agency will have a specialist recruiter for each technical area you are looking to recruit in. This may mean that you have multiple points of contact. You can address this by assigning someone from the agency to be the sole point of contact or account manager but bear in mind that recruiters like a personal connection to the hiring manager.

Depending on the complexity of the role/s, you want to make sure you agree on delivery goals that are achievable. Talk things through and ask your recruiter what you can realistically expect from them. Typically, a good recruiter should be able to find you two to three strong matches for one position in a couple of weeks. This may vary slightly considering the complexity of the role.

With these communication points in place, you should feel confident that both sides know what to expect from the process. Good communication is where much of the confidence of working together will come from. Ultimately, think of the recruiter as an extension of yourself – they will be representing you, your job and your company.

FOUR

The TALENT Method

After speaking with hundreds of business owners, I recognised that there is a lack of structure in their recruitment processes, especially when working with agencies. In response, I developed a unique method called TALENT that can be applied to any business to help streamline their recruitment process. The method details the stages an agency can follow to provide the best recruitment results. It is easy to follow and uses six core elements.

Each element is like a pillar supporting each part of the method – if you miss one part or complete it to a low standard then that pillar will crumble.

TALENT – an overview

Here is a brief introduction to each area which is explored in greater detail later in the chapter.

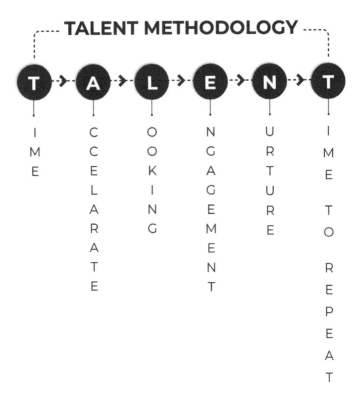

TALENT METHODOLOGY

T → A → L → E → N → T

T	A	L	E	N	T
I	C	O	N	U	I
M	C	O	G	R	M
E	E	K	A	T	E
	L	I	G	U	
	A	N	E	R	T
	R	G	M	E	O
	A		E		
	T		N		R
	E		T		E
					P
					E
					A
					T

T = Time

This is the important starting block. The agency will need to have certain information made available to understand and analyse what they are looking for, what's important and what's not in order to be able to help determine the most efficient process. This includes key areas that need to be considered and discussed before any further steps are taken.

It's vital to take the time to:

- Analyse the existing job specification

- Confirm the wording of the job title

- Understand the skill set

- Be clear on the technical skills required

- Define the tasks and responsibilities

- Invest in selling the vacancy

- Outline your work culture and values

- Detail the salary and benefits

- Assess your current interview process

- Outline your target market

A = Accelerate

After you have analysed your current position and situation, you should then look at how you can accelerate the process of standing out as an employer of choice. The problem here is that there are usually no solid agreements in place about what actions you are going to take after you have discussed the initial requirements. Your recruiter should be able to take in all of the points discussed and come up with suggestions that best fit your requirements. In tech recruitment, one of the key factors to success is *speed*. So, if the recruiter can come up with suggestions on how to streamline your process to make it faster, better results will be seen down the line.

L = Looking

This is the core function of what you are employing the recruiter to do. A recruiter should have several avenues to help you identify the right people for your business. Standard ones include LinkedIn and internal databases. What you'll want to see is that your recruiter is using all the resources available to make sure they are finding the best possible people they can for you. Specifically, I will uncover some areas where you can help your recruiter find hidden gems.

E = Engagement

This is probably the most pivotal part of the recruitment process but one that is often overlooked in terms of how to maximise your chances of securing the people you want and feeling confident about how your company is being advertised. It's really important to have a thorough grasp on how your company is being promoted to the top talent. I'll show you what you can do with your recruiter to improve your engagement with potential candidates, pique their interest and improve your response rate.

N = Nurture processes

Once you have engaged a candidate with the recruiter, the next step is to go through your process. The interview process for every business is usually unique. What you want to ensure is that your recruiter is in constant contact with the candidate throughout the process. This allows them to give you timely feedback and to be responsive and get the next step organised as soon as possible, assuming it's positive. The demand for tech professionals is incredibly high. In my experience, there are usually two jobs to every one candidate available, so it's highly likely that if they are talking to your business they will be talking to others. Your recruiter should be able to help you tailor your process, making it feel more personal and flexible, so you don't lose out to a competitor by being behind them in the recruitment process.

T = Time to repeat

Once you have come to the end of this method, it's essential to understand what has gone well and what has not so that you can consistently improve your process. This method should give you the right combination of results. Still, you will inevitably have to repeat it until you find the perfect candidate or whenever you have a new position to fill.

TALENT – a step-by-step guide

Now that you have a brief overview of the process, let's look at each step in detail.

Time

Making sure you take time to analyse the existing job specification with your recruiter at the beginning of your recruitment process is a critical step in making sure you and your recruiter are on the right track and everything is in place for a successful recruiting journey.

You want to feel confident that your recruiter knows about the vacant position in detail so that they are confident in what they are looking for in the market. Many tech managers assume that writing and sending a job description to a recruiter is enough for them to then go out and find someone suitable to fill the vacancy. They don't take the time to fully brief the recruiter on the position. This is like deciding that you are going to build a house, so you have an architect draw up the plans, then just hand the plans over to the builder and ask them to complete the building. The builder completes it based on what he can decipher from the drawings and the house you end up with is not quite what you had in mind. How did this happen? The plans were exact, the drawings clear, materials listed. Of course, to build a successful building the architect needs to sit down with the builder and discuss the plans. He needs to explain what each part is, why it's been designed in such a way, what materials to use and what the end result should look like. They have regular discussions to make sure that neither of them goes off track and that they are in agreement throughout the process. You would follow this plan for building a house and recruitment should be no different: you both want the same goal, which is a successful placement.

If your recruiter does not request to take time to be fully briefed about the position, this should be your first red flag in terms of working with them. I would be concerned about someone building a house for me if they did not speak to the architect, and the same should go for you when recruiting. You might see this as a big investment of your time that could be utilised elsewhere, but if you do not want to waste time and resources further down the line, it's vital you take the time now to discuss and analyse the job position together. As with building a house, laying the foundations is crucial. So, too, is setting out the parameters of your recruiting process. The only time a recruiter is able to work from a job spec alone (and you are able to give a minimal briefing) is when you have been working together for some time and the position is the same one you have recruited successfully for many times before. In this case, the recruiter probably knows what you are looking for better than you do. Even so, a short briefing is always helpful, especially if anything has changed, no matter how minor.

The best place to start with the analysis is to have already completed a basic written job description of what you are looking for. Send this to the recruiter at least a few days before your scheduled discussion together, so that they can digest the material. This way, the recruiter will already have an idea of what it is you want and how complex the role is. The more detailed you can be in your description, the better. Do not confuse this with putting together a wish list. Make sure you include only the essentials of what's required for the position. This job spec does not have to be perfect or the one you use for your own advertisement so don't worry about it looking good. At this stage it should just be for the eyes of you and the recruiter.

When a recruiter analyses the position with you, it is vital that they take the time to look closely at the following nine areas.

1. Confirm the wording of the job title

Make this as clear as possible. Avoid using vague terms such as 'Senior Software Engineer'. Be specific. If it's developing Android applications, title it as 'Senior Android Developer'; if it's developing Java, call it 'Java Developer', and so on. This may sound obvious, but some recruiters will just run a search based on a generalised job title (not the good ones, may I add) and you do not want to fall into this trap.

2. Understand the skill set

List the skills required for the job – try to keep this short. Only include the essential skills. Often referred to as the 'buzzwords', recruiters use these keywords when searching for your candidates. A good recruiter will challenge you on the skills and even try to trim them down. A good recruiter will be able to categorise these skills in the order of importance they are required for the position.

If you have other skills that are important but not critical, it's a good idea to break them into two categories of 'must have skills' and 'nice to have skills' so the recruiter knows what's essential, and what's not. Then you want to be clear on what level of experience you are looking for in each of those individual skills. This means the recruiter will be better able to analyse a candidate's profile to make sure they are ticking the right boxes, which increases the likelihood that they will find a strong candidate for you.

It can also be useful to inform the recruiter of your current tech stack within the business, but make sure you don't confuse this with the required skills. This is for information purposes only and helps paint a picture of what your tech environment looks like so that your recruiter can feel informed enough to explain more about the role to the candidates they speak with. You need to stress that these are *not* the primary skills they should be looking for.

3. Be clear on the technical skills required

When it comes to technical skills, you can often list a 'technology skill' which is part of a range of similar technologies. Having experience with one technology should be good enough to understand another, for example, databases. You might be using MySQL and so that's what the candidate will be working with in the position you have open, but in terms of the skills needed by the applicant, good relational database skills are sufficient. Tell your recruiter what type of category the skills are, for example, relational databases: 'We use MySQL. Ideally, we are looking for someone with experience in this but candidates who have worked with any other relational databases are welcome as the skill set should be easily transferable.' As a tech leader this may sound basic but it's important to be clear, so your recruiter pitches the job accurately.

From here you want to explain why a specific skill or technology is needed so the recruiter can understand its importance. For example, 'All of our backend is written in Java so it's essential for someone to have a strong working knowledge of Java.' Again, it may sound simple to someone with technical experience but giving the context of the position and detail of the skill set required really does help the recruiter understand what's needed and why. In turn, this enables them to find the most suitable candidate for the position and for your organisation.

4. Define tasks and responsibilities

Once you have gone through the necessary skills you then need to explain the responsibilities. This is another potential 'red flag' area where your recruiter may not get the full picture. You might list a set of tasks, for example:

i. Maintain our current product

ii. Develop new features

iii. Increase the performance

iv. Fix bugs

The problem with this description is that it's so high level that it doesn't give the recruiter a clear idea of what the daily work looks like or what's interesting about the new position. Before speaking with the recruiter, it's a good idea to sit down with your engineering team and ask them what's interesting about this role from their perspective. Engineers get excited about technical challenges, so the more specific you can be about the challenges this position will have, the better the recruiter will understand what the job entails so they can feel confident about selling these points to prospective candidates. For example, if you have 100,000 concurrent users and are solving tough scaling issues, then share it. Engineers love to know the specific challenges rather than the generic explanation of 'help develop new features' or 'maintain our existing legacy system'.

The clearer you can explain the project you are working on, the better. If you are able to make the recruiter feel excited about the position and your company, the more the recruiter will feel invested in what it is you are working towards, understand it and why it's interesting, so the better they will be able to sell the position and the company to prospective candidates.

TOP TIP

It can really help to sell a job by outlining some of the challenges your engineering team have recently overcome.

---

5. Invest in selling the vacancy

Following on from the tasks and responsibilities, you will also want your recruiter to be able to sell the company and your values. You want to be able to position your company as an attractive employer. Even if it's obvious, you still want to inform the recruiter of what your business does and what the core business model is. Following this basic information, you will then want to inform the recruiter *why* someone should be interested in working for your business. If you have any key selling points about the business, it's good to highlight them here. If you have lots of users, tell them the numbers. Are you partnered with a well-known brand? Tell them. Are you doing something different from your competitors? Tell them. Are you a start-up? Do you make lightning-quick decisions? Tell them! Give the recruiter as many appealing facts about the business as possible. But don't oversell. Give facts; don't sell dreams as this will leave everyone disappointed in the long run and potentially damage your brand.

6. Outline your work culture and values

Most candidates want to know what you stand for as a business. What are your values and what is your working culture like? Be sure to give details on the team size and how people work together. These are often common questions candidates will ask the recruiter prior to engaging in an interview process.

7. Detail the salary and benefits

You will want to be clear on salary and benefits. With salary, it's important you give the recruiter a range or budget to work with. The recruiter needs to understand what the maximum is that you will be happy to pay in order to avoid wasting anyone's time. Although technical people are not always driven by the money, salary is clearly an important part to any job. Most good tech engineers are well compensated and sometimes it's the number that will first catch the attention of an engineer. If you are able to pay above market average, you will have a better chance of securing the best talent. You're probably thinking, 'Well of course offering more money attracts more attention,' but it's not always about offering a big salary. I see a higher interest in positions which include a salary range. An experiment run by Stack Overflow[1] in 2016 reported that job listings with a salary range get 75% more clicks than job listings that do not.

Benefits are also important. If your company has a list of benefits alongside the salary, tell your recruiter about all of them. Most engineers will weigh up the total package rather than just the salary. Flexible working hours are most often in high demand. In my experience, the possibility of remote office options also tends to be high on the list of preferred requirements.

The recruiter should be able to combine this information and give you feedback as to where you sit in the market. They'll let you know if you are competitive and how this may affect their search for your candidate. This is where you can really start to separate the average recruiters from the good ones. If they are experienced, they should be able to give you this feedback instantly to help position you as a more attractive employer.

---

1   M Sherman, 'Salary Transparency At Stack Overflow' [blog post], The Overflow (July 2016), https://stackoverflow.blog/2016/07/27/salary-transparency/#75, accessed 14 October 2020

8. Assess your current interview process

Once the salary range is settled you will need to explain your internal interview process in detail. This is important as the recruiter will talk to both passive and active candidates. If the recruiter knows you have a few stages, they can advise you on how quickly you might need to act. If, for example, they present an active candidate, it's likely this candidate will be in other processes. If your process is at the start and the candidate is already in final talks with other businesses, then you know whether it makes sense to start a process. The recruiter should give you this information upfront, so you know what time scales you might need to move forward at and if you have the time to start a process and invest in this candidate or not. Candidates often ask what the process is and the recruiter should be able to lay out the expectations from the start.

9. Outline your target market

The recruiter should now have enough to start a detailed search to yield you the best results. At this stage, if you want to give your recruiter a head start it can be useful to point out where most of your current team has come from so that the recruiter can get an idea of the type of people you have hired before. If you already have a few people from an industry area (or maybe even a particular company) that interest you then give your recruiter a list of good places to start looking. Ultimately, the recruiter wants to pinpoint the people you like and get you results fast, so the more targets you can give them the better.

Overall, this stage takes the most amount of time so it's really worth investing the time upfront to ensure your recruiter has all the information they need. When these early briefings are done correctly, this will be the biggest time-saver in the whole recruitment process. The recruiter should be able to bring back highly suitable candidates if the requirements are realistic. Do bear in mind, however, that there is no guarantee of a shortlist of all A-star candidates – the market can often dictate what's available to your requirements. You will find that you might have to finetune certain parts of your 'wish list' when you realise you don't need something, or you can drop a 'must have' requirement to a 'nice to have' as you go through the process. If you are dealing with an experienced recruiter, they will be able to tell you straight away if your ideal candidate is possible to find, and if not, which requirements you might need to consider changing. You want to work with a recruiter who will challenge you on what you are looking for if you are going to be realistic in hiring, especially if it's an urgent or critical hire.

'Time' to analyse is a great starting point to set you on track to a strong collaboration together. In summary, be sure that you cover all nine stages:

1. Confirm the wording of the job title
2. Understand the skill set, including technical skills, required
3. Be clear on the tasks and responsibilities
4. Invest in selling the vacancy
5. Outline your work culture and values
6. Detail the salary and benefits
7. Assess your current interview process
8. Advertising/targeting
9. Outline your target market

Once you have been working with a recruiter for a while, you can skip some of these parts as they will often remain the same, but no matter how comfortable you get with your recruiter, for each position you hire (and unless it is a carbon copy of one you have done before) you should still have a briefing discussion with them to make sure you are both crystal clear on what you are looking for.

Accelerate

With recruitment being so time consuming and job adverts everywhere, it's important to consider in what areas you can stand out from the crowd to accelerate your chances of getting noticed by A-players.

There are two practical areas that are good to focus on to optimise your process: video and meet-ups. And then, of course, there's literally being faster and beating your competitors to it.

1. Video content

This is becoming increasingly important in recruitment and for good reason. Video can convey a message quickly – some people feel that it's less work to watch rather than read. It adds personality to a message – the candidate immediately has some visual clues into your company. People are increasingly using the YouTube search as part of their internet search.[2] The reason I feel video is so important is that it has so many applications, it's so easy to do, is accessible and can really help add a personal touch to your whole recruitment drive. People want to feel connected to your business before applying or going through a recruitment process.

TOP TIP

Showing your recruiter a five-minute video about your business can be more effective than an hour-long discussion or a carefully crafted job specification.

---

2   Global Reach, 'The 2nd Largest Search Engine On The Internet', www.globalreach.com/blog/2020/01/28/the-2nd-largest-search-engine-on-the-internet, accessed 16 November 2020

Videos are a great way to showcase your business – to give someone a feeling about your work culture and what you're all about. A recruiter likes to be armed with as much information as possible and they can use a video for their own information or share it with candidates.

Even if you invite your recruiter into the office or if they have been there plenty of times before they can sometimes lose memory of what it's like to actually be there. This helps jog their memory and can also be used by them when they are trying to headhunt a candidate or engage someone's interest.

One way to make video really engaging for your candidates is to make some short clips to welcome them and explain your process, then have these emailed to them on the interview confirmations. The content should be to the point and no longer than two to three minutes overall so the recipient doesn't simply click it off. To start, welcome the candidate and thank them for taking the time to apply. Make them feel special and share that you are just as excited about the interview as they probably are. Give them a brief introduction about who you are and why this position is important for your business. From there, give them a quick overview of what to expect from the interview and what the typical process looks like. Include anyone they may meet along the way so that they are well informed of what to expect.

Additionally, you can have an introduction to the business or maybe a tour of the office on your website. The clip sent to them can be a great opportunity to suggest that they look at this before the interview. This tactic allows you to quickly test how interested in or motivated for the position they are, according to whether they bother to take the time to view the clip or not. I've found from my own business surveys that this approach really helped engage candidates, with 94% of them stating that they felt more connected to the business before even speaking to anyone.

Videos may seem a little scary at first and you may feel like you have to make a hundred takes to get the perfect one, but the beauty of video is that you can really have fun with it, and it will help bring out your personality and what the business is about. If you are looking for inspiration, one of the best recruitment videos I have seen was by a company called SodaStream.[3] If you do decide to make a public video and it's done well, it even has the power to go viral and super-boost your brand image. One company we worked with produced a short recruitment video and shared it on some of the most popular social media sites. The applications for their open positions went through the roof, over a 500% increase overnight.

---

3   SodaStream Recruitment, www.youtube.com/watch?v= 0z6MVBT4hSw, accessed 20 October 2020

An additional advantage of using video is that it encourages sharing. People often feel naturally compelled to share well-crafted video content and it's a great way for you to spread your job advertisement quickly. Video is also great for mobile as it's convenient for people to watch on their smartphones. In fact, mobile video usage has increased by almost ten million daily viewing minutes in the last few years,[4] and that number is showing no signs of slowing.

Video is a great way to headhunt candidates and something I would encourage. Most candidates usually receive an email or LinkedIn message regarding a job proposal, which is what everyone else is doing. Writing an email or message pitching your job is becoming normal and boring unless you have a quirky way to stand out or have a skill in pitching over email to gain interest. To really stand out, I've found sending a short video message to a candidate shows that I've spent time reviewing their profile and am not just spamming people. The more personal you can make the video the more likely you are to receive a reply as the candidate will feel you have reached out to them specifically so will feel more inclined to respond.

---

4   J Mawhinney, '50 Visual Content Marketing Statistics You Should
     Know In 2020' [blog post], HubSpot (updated August 2020),
     https://blog.hubspot.com/marketing/visual-content-marketing
     -strategy, accessed 14 October 2020

TOP TIP

A personalised video message is much harder to ignore, delete or forget compared to a generic email.

However, beware as, like job specifications, recruitment videos can end up being generic and boring too. So when creating your short video be sure to make it stand out – make it quirky, fun or memorable. The more unique you can be, the more engaging the video will be for the user. Ultimately, video works as humans are visual creatures. Visual storytelling helps us to better comprehend and retain information and is the format that's most likely to pique a new hire's interest. According to an article by TechCrunch,[5] *one billion hours* of content are watched on YouTube around the world *per day*. This is exactly why it shouldn't be overlooked when you are developing your organisation's recruitment strategy to help you (and your recruiter) win more suitable candidates.

2. Meet-ups

The second way to stand out and a great way to get in contact with your local tech engineering community is to sign up for local meet-up groups. Look for websites

---

5   D Etherington, 'People Now Watch 1 Billion Hours Of YouTube Per Day', TechCrunch (February 2017), https://tcrn.ch/2HoeLfZ, accessed 25 October 2020

where you can connect and interact with likeminded people to discuss specific topics. Meet-ups can range from hobbies to work interests such as programming and should be part of your recruitment strategy to connect and interact with potential candidates who are local to you. They give you an 'in' to get to know your local tech community. While the majority of people who attend meet-ups are not actively looking for new positions, they are often a great way to introduce your business to people and start piquing interest in your company so that they could end up applying to your open positions.

Meet-ups are often a good way to identify people with a specific niche skill or technology you might be looking for. If you find a meet-up group that is relevant to your business with a technology that you are using, you should make an effort to attend and network. It is also a great idea to see how you can use your office space as the location for a meet-up. This is a great way for people to get in touch with your business and can encourage them to be interested in considering a position with you, albeit as a secondary tactic.

If you host a meet-up and it continues to grow, you can also start reaching out to speakers to talk at the meet-up. Typically, most people who are confident enough to hold a public talk on a tech subject are usually the ones who are in the top percentage of experts in that area and these are the A-players you ideally want in your tech team.

This is more of a long-game approach. By reaching out to people at your meet-up, you establish a connection without 'recruitment' ever being mentioned. The A-players get hit more than most when it comes to recruitment and trying to recruit them straight away would be a sure-fire way of turning them off. Meet-ups give you the opportunity to build up rapport with 'unreachable' candidates and the opportunity to approach them after time. Building rapport takes time so this is not a short-term solution. But perhaps your business is better suited to the long game? If you know that you have an ongoing requirement for a particular skill set as a business, building long-term links with known specialist talent in the trade is worthwhile.

TOP TIP

Most tech candidates we speak to often state wanting to work with other talented people as one of their key motivators for joining a new business.

If you can attract and secure some of the well-known tech guys in your area, this in itself will attract other great engineers to want to work with you. This will also bring more tech kudos to your business and make your recruitment task so much easier.

If you are unable to host, an alternative way to generate interest in your business or open positions is to invest in geo-targeted advertising via Facebook. Facebook remains the largest social network and is most likely to be on the phones of *all* the people who attend tech events. Drop a pin on Facebook and advertise your role in targeted Facebook feeds. This can also be a really useful tactic to be deployed at tech conferences where you might want to generate interest. You are likely to get applications from people who might be from all corners of the world and who have never heard about your business before.

What you have to remember when you have a recruit-ment campaign is that not every person will be on one platform. Heck, some engineers actually deactivate their LinkedIn profiles as they get hit with too many 'opportunities'. In today's market, you have to be more creative with how you are going to identify people and meet-ups are a great way to get introduced to those hidden gems who are not always so visible on social media. In addition, investing in geo-targeting ads to where meet-ups or conferences are happening and advertising there will help increase applications and be a worthwhile investment.

3. Speed

One of the critical factors of success is speed, so once you have created some ways to stand out you need to look at optimising your process with your recruiter. If you have more than one job position you are hiring for, then set the job positions into an A and B list, where A is critical priority and B is lower priority. For example:

Priority A SLA:

- Agree on the delivery date of profiles that are reasonable to the position's complexity.

- Respond to one another on applicant information communication within twenty-four hours.

- Respond to all applicants within three working days.

- Set a minimum of three to five working days between interview stages for applicants.

- Recruiter provides applicant interview feedback within twenty-four hours.

- You provide feedback to the recruiter within twenty-four hours.

- Once an offer is delivered, follow up with a contract on the same working day.

Priority B SLA:

- If you have priority A positions, ask the recruiter not to focus on these but keep an eye open and not to set a delivery date.

- Respond to one another on applicant information communication within two days.

- Respond to all applicants within five working days.

- Set a minimum of three to five working days between interview stages for applicants.

- Recruiter provides applicant interview feedback within twenty-four hours.

- You provide feedback to the recruiter within twenty-four hours.

- Once an offer is delivered, follow up with a contract on the same working day.

You will notice that there are minimal differences between A and B positions. This is because you still want the process to work as efficiently as possible when you have an applicant in process. The applicant will not be aware of what the priority of that position is within the company. You should aim to treat all applicants within a process at the same level of urgency – the main difference is that if the position is a lower priority, you will not want your recruiter to focus on it until you have closed the priority A job positions.

This way, your recruiter is likely to be far more pro-ductive; however, you should not completely stop your recruiter from working on the priority B positions as it's likely they may come across someone in their network or within passing discussions. Just because the job is not super urgent does not mean you should miss out on excellent talent when it's available to you from the recruiter.

Having a clear overview of the process expectations from both sides will help you streamline your systems and so accelerate towards securing top talent for your position.

Looking

A key part of the TALENT method is for your recruiter to have a clear plan on what they are looking for, enabling them to come up with a market map. It's important to plan and map out your targets and there are things your recruiter should be doing to identify prime targets for your business. A market map is quite simply a plan of action. You'll note the specific areas you are going to target to pinpoint a higher success rate and yield a higher return of candidates who should be suitable for your business. This is broken down into three significant parts: internal, external and technical.

1. Internal

Internal starts with looking at your existing team and breaking down where they have worked before. It also considers who they might be connected with, which will enable you to gain some quick wins to bring people in. Most companies offer an incentive for employees to refer people they know who could be suitable for the business, but if they know too many people it's hard for them to pinpoint anyone unless you are specific.

For example, I've played football for the majority of my life. I have met plenty of great players along the way who I have either played with or against. If you were to ask me to recommend someone from one of the teams off the top of my head, I might be able to think of one or two but that's about it. However, if someone approached me and mentioned the names of specific players, I would then quickly be able to tell you if I thought they were a good player or not. The same theory applies for asking your existing team who they have worked with before. This is a great way to target closely connected people and build a strong shortlist internally, or something you can ask your recruiter to conduct with your team.

The best place to do this is on LinkedIn. Ask your team to bring up their LinkedIn profiles and make a list of all the companies they have worked at before. Now keyword search the type of skill you are looking for inside the selected businesses that your existing employees have worked at before, for example, Java.

This should bring up a list of all the people inside those businesses who have working experience with Java. Through LinkedIn's ranking system you should be able to see who is a first, second or third connection. You want to aim for the second connections as these are likely to be people who your employees are connected with or have worked with before. Repeat this keyword search for all the previous companies they have worked for, which should return a long list. From here, speak to the employees to identify which individuals (if any) would be a good fit for the business.

This is where you can ask your employees for introductions to people – you are more likely to receive a warm welcome from a solicited approach than reaching out to them out of the blue. A good way to start the conversation is to say, 'I'm a connection of 'employee's name'. I understand you know each other or have worked together before and I've heard good things about you. We'd love to get in touch with you to see how open you are to having an informal conversation about a role we have here that we'd love to run past you.' In my experience, this approach to headhunting receives a 90% response rate compared to a standard, 'Are you open to a new opportunity?' message.

LinkedIn also has a feature where you can endorse people for their skills. This can be a great place to look as people typically endorse other people who have a skill in common. If we keep with the same example, using Java as the main skill, look at your employee's existing endorsements and see if they also have a list of people who have endorsed them for that skill. Then, follow the same process as before in creating a long list and editing it into a shortlist. People who endorse others on LinkedIn are likely to have a closer connection to that person and have seen their work before, which again increases your chances of getting a response from a message.

To go one step further you can also look at written recommendations on LinkedIn. Check your employee's recommendations – if someone has taken the time to write a review or recommendation on someone, it's highly likely that they hold the closest connection to your employee. Again, you will be able to leverage that relationship in your message to them, as well as asking your current employee's thoughts on that person being suitable for your business.

The internal market map strategy is the most effective way to build a significant list of people to approach who have the right skill set and will most likely be suitable for open positions. As the saying goes, 'good people like to work with good people'. By implementing this alone you might have enough resources to go on without having to use the other two strategies.

If you're thinking, 'We want to recruit people for a new team where we don't have any expertise,' or, 'I don't have that many people in my existing team,' or perhaps, 'My team does not have big networks on their LinkedIn to use,' then fear not – this is where the other two areas will help you to map a market of good candidates.

2. External

External looks at your competitors. As a business owner you should have a clear picture of who your direct competitors are. It's worthwhile putting this list together so that your recruiter can target people from those businesses. Of course, you want to be tactful on how you approach this with your recruiter, and I do not recommend targeting businesses where you have a personal connection. If you start messaging every employee from your competitor at the same time, it won't take long for it to reach the ears of someone in management who will not appreciate your targeted approach. This can create bad blood between both companies and may lead them to returning the same approach in trying to headhunt your staff. The best way is to approach this in stages. Try to identify only the key people that are likely to be the best fit for your business. I find it best to break it down into two sections. Spend some time on LinkedIn researching each profile and put the top matches in your first list that you will reach out to immediately. Leave the others in another list that you can reach out to in a few weeks' time or stage it by reaching out to two or three people weekly.

After you have exhausted a list of all your direct competitors, create a list of industry competitors. While these companies will not be exactly the same as yours, they are in the same industry area and are likely to also have people with the skills you need. For example, if you are a FinTech business, you might want to explore the different types of businesses in the finance industry (banks, insurance, etc).

This is great way to identify lots of people. The only way you are going to narrow this down is to start talking with these individuals to see how suitable they may be. It's probably a longer way to find people but should still produce a good map of places to find relevant people.

3. Technical

Technical looks at the tech stack competitors you have. Within your market, it's possible you will know companies that use a similar tech stack where you are likely to find people with transferable skills. The best way to do this is to write a list of technical buzzwords that you have in your company and copy that into LinkedIn in your local area to see who else might be working with those technologies. This is likely to bring up a long list and the only way to shorten this is to go out and start talking to people. Once you have identified a business with similar technologies that might work, you then want to dive into who is working there. Narrow this down to people who have the matching keyword or position in their profile. To understand if they are really going to be suitable, you must read their whole profile.

Ultimately, it's good to implement all three methods so you can bring up a long enough list to keep you busy with a good amount of target people to get in contact with. Internal is my personal favourite as it's a lot more successful than the other two and encourages engagement from your existing team to help with your recruitment strategy. Whichever way you choose, I've found these three the best ways to create your target market map and to get you in the position to start your headhunting or recruitment campaign.

Searching is the key part in the process. Along with creating a market map, this will be your key ingredient to identifying candidates. There are many avenues that you can use to source candidates. When asking your recruiter what tools they use they find candidates, make sure these bases are covered so you know you are getting the best selection of candidates available.

Engagement

The engagement process is the procedure used to attract someone to a position.

It starts with the first interaction you have with the candidate and should be led by your recruiter. Remember that recruiters should be saving you a lot of time during the search and selection phase as this will be the majority of what you are paying them for, but you should be aware of what they're doing to attract, initiate and engage potential candidates. Not doing so can damage your brand and your attempts to attract the right people for your job.

The first step is addressing the shortlist of potential candidates that you have drawn up from the searching part of the process. First impressions count, especially if you and your recruiter are trying to headhunt someone. Tech people are in high demand and are often approached several times a day with an 'amazing opportunity'. *Please* don't be the person who uses this as the subject line or first part of a message to someone. Everyone has an 'amazing opportunity', but how do you know it's an amazing opportunity for them before you have even spoken to them? If you are unable to speak to someone face-to-face or on the phone (the preferred method to first engage with someone), the worst thing you can do is send them a mediocre message that looks as if it has been copied and pasted to as many candidates as possible. It's clichéd and a pet hate in the tech community but a method many recruiters unfortunately still adopt.

No one likes feeling they are being spammed. Make sure you have read their profile in full and when messaging, make your approach personal. Explain why you feel their profile would be a really strong fit for your position. Take the time to fill out the message with noteworthy achievements – mention why they caught your attention. For example, have they listed a group they are part of? Great, mention that. Have they studied at a university which is relevant to your position? Great, mention that. The more personal you can make the introductory part of the message, the more likely you are to receive a response. Yes, it takes longer, and you have to think about what you are writing, but just being another person that sends them a message with high-level sales jargon will get you nowhere or straight into the junk folder. It may even burn that bridge for the future. You must stand out – for all the right reasons.

The best way to connect with a potential candidate is to reference someone you both know in the introduction as these are the first few lines that will be read. If it's relevant they will read on with interest. As discussed already, you could be creative and send them a personal video message, a great alternative if you are not a fan of writing.

Now you have captured this individual's attention, you need to describe what you have on offer. The danger here is not to fall into a typical sales pitch where you list what *you* assume is interesting about the opportunity. Without speaking to someone, you can't sell anything effectively. People buy when you have something *they* actually want. The only way you can uncover that is by first questioning and understanding what they are looking for and then you can sell to either the interests or motivations that align with what you can offer. The key is not to sell yet, but to give a good overview of what the business does. Then detail the tasks or challenges you are currently facing, followed by the skills you need and why you think their profile would be suitable. It's best to state facts here. To close off the message, you want to show your candidate what's in it for them. This is not always just a list of benefits the company has. This is a good place to highlight what they could be a part of – the more specific and technical you can be, the better.

TOP TIP

Most of the tech people I have spoken to over the years list a technical challenge as being one of the key drivers for considering a new position.

This is not a golden formula for success, but this approach is likely to give you a response, which is the goal of the introductory message. If you do get a response, you have done the job well. If you have written the introduction message well enough, even with a negative response people will most likely thank you for investing the time and appreciate the effort you have made to contact them. This is more likely to open them up to keeping in touch for the future. It is also a great way to build your network so you create more connections in common for other candidates you might want to approach in the future, as well as keeping them as a warm contact to possibly re-approach when the timing or position could be more suitable.

Assuming you get a positive response, you then want to engage with that person. For the candidate this is the start of the journey they will have with you, so it's important to start off well and to ensure that the recruiter gives the candidate a positive and professional impression from the beginning.

The best way to do this is to have an open conversation with the candidate. Start with an informal chat. Kick off with short introductions and then ask them about their experience. Ask questions about their skills in relation to the position to analyse whether the role seems suitable. Assuming they match the requirements well, you then want to dive into what's interesting and important to them as well as what's missing from their current role. This is where you can start to sell – you take their points and sell them the things your opportunity has that align with them. The more things you can match up with theirs, the more likely they will be to continue with the process.

Nurture process

The nurturing process is the procedure of ensuring you look after the applicants throughout all aspects of the interview and recruitment process. Preparation is key.

While everyone agrees that an interview process should be structured in a way that best suits the business, many forget that the interview process should be the best experience possible for the candidate as well – you need to nurture them through your recruitment process. Whether you hire or not, you want every person who walks through your door to leave wanting your job and feeling that your company is the place to be. This is what many companies don't do well – they forget to sell their business and the position. They tend to think that the person being interviewed should do all the hard work.

Consider this for a second: if you could have one person walk through your door who you truly admire and would love to work with (perhaps someone famous or the person who invented the technology your company works with), how differently would you approach the interview? I am guessing you would be trying really hard to impress that person and be selling the position to them tenfold. This is the mindset you should have from the start of every interview. I guarantee this will increase your ability to secure people and reduce the amount of people who you might offer the position to but who decline it. By tweaking your approach, you will also get a good reputation in the market and more referrals.

1. Putting the candidate first

If you have a standout recruitment process and an interview strategy that puts the candidate first, you will gain more traction with people who might not have thought about applying before. On the flip side, if you have a bad recruitment and interview process where you are just grilling the candidate and then giving no feedback, think about what that does for your reputation. I've spoken to plenty of good candidates about a position and had them simply reject the idea of an interview due to negative information they have received from a friend or a platform like Glassdoor.

While you should make sure you set the bar high, there is still plenty of room to make the interview enjoyable for the candidate in question. Let's face it – most people don't enjoy an interview where they are bombarded with questions or asked to do tasks under pressure (for example, people watching everything you do in a coding session – a completely unnatural situation in a tech working environment). If you can make it interactive and encourage the candidates to lead part of the interview you will make them feel that it's more of a conversation. You are more likely to see the real person come through in the interview, ideally yielding you better results and giving you a better reflection of that person.

2. Having a collaborative process

With most companies, HR is often involved from the start. While it's essential that they are, it's best to keep them overseeing the process rather than controlling it. HR does not feel the pain as much as hiring managers do and without the same level of urgency and recruitment being only a part of their workload, a bottleneck can be created and slow down your process.

As you move into the deeper part of the interview process, the hiring manager should take over but remember to keep the recruiter involved as they still have a big part to play. Too many businesses seem to think there are two sides here, which is wrong. You need to work together. You should still make the process as collaborative as possible – you want the recruiter to be involved so that when it comes to discussing feedback (positive or negative), the recruiter can then use that information to streamline their further searches for you. This will also help enhance the process to make sure everything runs as smoothly as possible regarding the candidate experience.

3. Keep it moving

It's important for your interview process to be quick as good people don't hang around for jobs and do not enjoy jumping through multiple hoops over a long period of time. Even a powerhouse like Google had to reduce their recruitment process: the effect of their long process was that everyone in Silicon Valley had a bad experience story to share about them and inevitably more people questioned whether to apply. This type of knock-on effect can cause a business to miss out on exceptional people. Google changed their process as soon as they recognised that a company has hundreds of jobs, but a person only has one, so it's important to put them first.[6]

---

6   Laszlo Bock, *Work Rules! Insights From Inside Google That Will Transform How You Live And Lead* (John Murray, 2016)

This is exactly how you should view it: put yourself in the candidate's shoes, scrutinise every part of your process and make it better where possible. Typically, a two or three stage process should provide enough touch points to be able to make an effective decision about a candidate over a two- to four-week period. Anything longer and you run the risk of your candidate losing interest or you lose out to the competition. Get your recruiter to inform a candidate of this process from start to finish upfront – this will also prompt the candidate to inform the recruiter if they have anything else in the pipeline.

4. Feeling connected

A common mistake is companies making their first step in the process for tech positions a technical task. While conducting a test or task to assess someone's skill level is important and should be a part of your process, it should *not* be at the start of your interaction. People first want to feel connected to the company and you want them to feel encouraged to do the task. Sending out a tech task at the beginning can start things off on the wrong foot. It screams, 'I don't trust your CV or what the recruiter has said about you.' First, make the time to have a short telephone or video chat with them. If your recruiter has done a good job, then this should be a part of the process that is more for them than you. It gives them the opportunity to fall in love with what it is you're doing and make them super keen about taking the next step.

5. Be clear

Another common mistake is that a surprising number of candidates come out of the first interview knowing little about the actual job apart from what's been written on the job spec. In any first interview, it is your responsibility to make sure the candidate knows exactly what the job entails and what the key challenges will be. Allow at least ten to fifteen minutes of the interview for this.

This is your opportunity to 'sell your position' – even if it turns out the candidate is not suitable; you want them to love what you do. Remember, your ultimate goal is to have a super-motivated candidate who can't wait to take the next step with you and who knows whether they feel they are suitable for the position. If you do this well then candidates who decide it might not be right for them may refer someone else to you.

6. It's a whole process

It's important to nurture your candidate throughout the *whole* recruitment process, not just the actual interview. The main reason interview processes take so long is not the interview itself – it's the feedback and the time between interviews that often cause the problem. Two things happen if the period between the first and second interview is too long. First, the candidate's motivation levels peak from the interview and rather than letting them ride the wave of this motivation by booking the next meeting quickly, if left too long, this motivation steadily declines. Second, you open up the opportunity for someone else, possibly one your competitors, to swoop in and secure them from right under your nose.

After the interview, take some time to make some notes on the candidate straight away. If you are already 100% sure the candidate looks like a great fit, get the ball rolling as soon as you can. I think it's good to let things settle and take some time to digest the interview so perhaps review your notes the following morning, adding or removing anything relevant, and then share them with your recruiter. This is also where you want your recruiter to step back in with detailed feedback from the candidate. If your recruiter does not do this, I would question what value they are actually bringing to the process apart from sourcing a CV.

Your recruiter should make a point of obtaining feedback from the candidate either straight after the interview or within twenty-four hours when it's fresh in their memory. It's also a great opportunity for the recruiter to uncover any other opportunities the candidate might have on the go, so you know where you stand. It's becoming increasingly common for companies to offer 'exploding offers' where the candidate needs to make a decision within a deadline, or the offer expires. A recruiter is important at this point as they will act as your middleman. They will uncover details you may not have been able to as the candidate will feel more at ease speaking about things they liked or disliked with someone who is impartial. The recruiter can relay what the candidate is actually thinking, and assuming it's a candidate you would like to move forward with, the details on what might be important for you to cover in the next meeting or areas that have been highlighted as a concern. If your recruiter uncovers an 'exploding offer', they can advise you on time scales so that you can respond accordingly.

Typically, in most tech interviews the next stage would be some form of an assignment related to the job. Now this is tricky territory. You can either request that the candidate complete the assignment in their own time or combine it with the second interview. Both are equally acceptable.

You want to make sure that the assignment is not going to take too long. In my experience, a tech task that takes a few hours is what most candidates are comfortable with – anything longer and the candidate loses motivation. Bear in mind that this assignment has to fit in with their lives. If a candidate already works full-time (which most A-player candidates do), most will struggle to find the time to complete it, especially if they have a family.

When setting the content of your tech assignment, make sure that it is closely aligned with what the person will be doing in their day-to-day tasks. With the tech assignment itself, the most common problem people have with it is that the task is entirely irrelevant to the skills you have listed for the job. It's about getting the right balance here. You don't want to make a task so relevant that you create the impression that the candidate is completing a piece of work for you for free.

Bringing a candidate in to do a tech task is an excellent opportunity to get them to feel your culture and working environment but you do not want to make them feel awkward. One of the biggest bug-bears technical candidates have is being asked to perform the task with people watching them. This is not something you would have in the real world and puts the candidate under immense and unnecessary pressure. Set them up on a desk close to the team they could potentially be working with or in a quiet office space, then give them a time frame and let them complete the task independently. It will put them at ease and provide them with the opportunity to show you their skills instead of being in a high-pressure environment that encourages mistakes.

TOP TIP

For a technical test, replicate a normal working situation as much as possible.

Once complete, you can then take some time analysing it and asking them questions. After the tech task, you should have some excellent information about the candidate, and they should have the right amount of information to start making an informed decision about you and how your business works and what the role will entail.

The second interview is also your opportunity to dig deeper and assess how good the fit is and whether the candidate aligns with your culture and team. From here, I advise bringing HR and other team members more into the interview process to help you make decisions.

Once all of these steps are complete, you and the candidate should be at the point of making a decision about working together. If you start to introduce more interviews at this stage, their motivation levels will drop significantly (see the graph below):

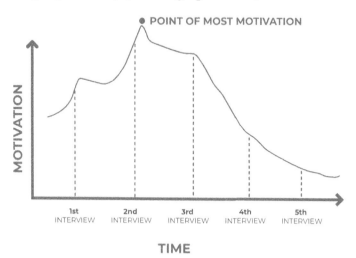

Figure 4.2 Interest levels during interview process

After the second interview, you will want to repeat the feedback stage. You want to make sure your recruiter is prompt with getting feedback from the interview while the candidate's motivation is now probably closest to its highest point. At this stage, you want the recruiter to pre-close the candidate so that they can report back to you with the input, and assuming things are positive from your side, what will make the candidate likely to accept an offer. At this point, your recruiter is acting as a broker to make both sides happy – this is an invaluable role.

The expectations of the candidate should have already been clearly laid out to you, the employer, from the beginning of the process. Your recruiter should re-evaluate and confirm these at this stage. However, it's always possible for the candidate to have spoken with other companies during the interview stage (although if you are following the guidance here, you will have eliminated this danger by moving more quickly than your competition) and so may have other offers on the table. If this is the case, your recruiter should do their best to uncover what these are and advise you accordingly so you can remain competitive. There is a common misconception here that if the money expectations from the candidate change in the latter stages of the process, the external recruiter is only trying to increase their fee (assuming it's on a percentage). This is not always accurate – by this point the recruiter is trying to make sure things happen by aligning everyone's expectations. If the recruiter *is* just trying to increase their fee, I share a useful tip later to combat this.

The next stage is making an offer. This is also a part of the process you want to make sure happens swiftly after the second/final interview – it should take no longer than a day. You should already have contracts prepared with minor changes to make in terms of adding personal details, salary, start date, etc.

Many companies make the error of making the offer directly without speaking to the recruiter first. Remember, your recruiter is your broker here. It's essential to run it past your recruiter first to eliminate the risk of delivering an offer that is not in line with the candidate's expectations and undo all the excellent work of getting to this point. Once the recruiter has delivered the candidate's feedback and you have made your decision (assuming it's positive), give your recruiter a quick call first to see what they think of the offer you want to put forward.

TOP TIP

The best way to feel comfortable that your recruiter has your best interests at heart regarding fees is to lock in the price based on the first offer you make (as long as this is not a ridiculously low offer otherwise your recruiter will feel you are trying to get out of paying a reasonable fee).

Your recruiter should know what the candidate is prepared to accept by pre-closing them and so can advise you on what to offer. This prevents needless negotiations. Most people don't enjoy a negotiation, so if you can make sure you get it right in the first attempt, your chance of securing that person will significantly increase. From the candidate's perspective, they feel they have been listened to, respected, are highly valued and that you and your company are serious about securing their signature. This is far better than having to go into a negotiation battle – sometimes negotiations end in a contract but do not give the working relationship the best of starts.

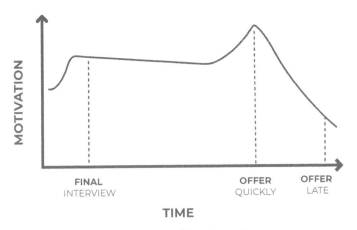

Figure 4.3 Making the offer

Once you have successfully agreed to work together, you head into a danger zone that can sometimes be overlooked. This is the point of time between a candidate accepting an offer and them handing in their resignation. It is becoming increasingly common for anyone in a tech job to receive a counteroffer. No company likes to lose a good employee, especially someone good at tech as they are often invaluable to a business. You should expect a counteroffer regardless of how well your process has gone and even if a candidate has initially agreed to work with you.

The best way to combat this and reduce the possibility of the candidate accepting a counteroffer is to cover it head-on at your offer stage, either directly or by asking your recruiter to do it. What you want is for your candidate to be aware that this may happen and try to get a verbal commitment that there is nothing their current company can do to keep them, so when their current company makes them a counteroffer, they have already subconsciously rejected it.

Of course, this won't always work as you are dealing with people – and people can change their minds. If you do head into a situation where the candidate is considering accepting a counteroffer, make sure you have had the opportunity to speak to them again before they make their decision. Remind them of their motivations to move positions in the first place and why this opportunity was right for them. Regardless of any counteroffer, in most cases these motivations won't have changed, which should then lean the decision in your favour again. Get the facts of the counteroffer and then, assuming you can, adjust your offer to trump the initial counteroffer.

This is why it's valuable to have a recruiter in place. Once a candidate has accepted an offer, your recruiter should know when the candidate plans to hand in their resignation and organise to have a follow-up call with them so they can then get details and stress-test the commitment to your offer. If the candidate does consider staying, do not let your ego get in the way. Reassure them they are making the right choice to come to you. You want your candidate to be 100% certain that they want to work for you. Bear in mind that leaving a business is difficult and can be emotional (especially if they have been with a company for a long time). They are also leaving a secure job, which is always a risk due to the probation period.

Once this is taken care of, you will want to stay in touch with the candidate at regular intervals to make sure things run smoothly and then start introducing them to an onboarding process, which is usually covered by HR. If you don't have an onboarding process or someone responsible for it, I highly suggest you get someone to do it and put one in place. After you have done all this hard work to make the recruitment process remarkable, you will want to make sure this is matched with a thorough and welcoming onboarding process. There is nothing worse than being made to feel like a number, or worse, forgotten, after signing a contract. The more fuss you can make about someone starting, the more integral and welcome they will feel.

By following the engagement and nurturing processes, you will find that exciting things will start to happen. As the tech community often moves in the same circles, people will start talking about you and your brand. Your reputation in the market will slowly increase and you will begin to get more direct applications and referrals, even referrals from candidates you didn't hire. If you take the time to make someone feel special in this process, you will be amazed at what some people will do for you without you even having to ask.

Time to repeat

Once you have come to the end of your recruiting process, it's essential to understand what has gone well and what has not so that you can continually improve your practices. If you follow the procedures outlined here, you should get positive results. Inevitability, you will need to tweak practices to find the perfect candidate or repeat the process to fill a new position.

PART THREE
ADDING VALUE

FIVE

Rocket Fuel Your Recruitment

This chapter looks at specific parts that you can ask your recruiter to add to the recruitment process to give it some rocket fuel, as well as giving you some useful hints and tips to make your contribution the best it can be. It will focus on:

- Preparation: Why it's essential, what you should be doing, and why your recruiter needs to get the candidate to prepare.

- Regular updates: Making the most of your and your recruiter's time and ensuring that you are working together.

- The pillars: A solid structure and critical bits of feedback information your recruiter should cover inside-out to give you the real lowdown on a candidate.

- Counteroffers: an in-depth look into these and some useful questions to pose to a candidate to further increase your chances of securing them.

- Making the offer: how to add some sparkle to an offer and deliver it at the perfect time.

Preparation

I have to start this section off with one of my favourite quotes, often attributed to Benjamin Franklin: 'By failing to prepare, you are preparing to fail.' Preparing before an interview is just as important for you as it is for your candidate. You are probably thinking, 'What? Why do I have to prepare for an interview I'm conducting? I've done this interview a thousand times; I know what I'm doing.' This circles back to a common theme throughout this whole book, and that is to turn the philosophy of interviewing on its head by putting the candidate before yourself or the company. By doing this small thing, you can make someone's interview experience so much more enjoyable. It will build up rapport super-fast, allowing candidates to instantly feel relaxed and able to open up to you quickly so you can assess if they are going to be the right person for the job and fit for your company. It also makes it more enjoyable for you and makes every interview different.

Typically, most managers review the CV and notes from their recruiter a few minutes before an interview and then ask questions based on the information they have in front of them. This approach is OK, but this only gives you the knowledge the candidate wants you to see and doesn't give you much information to connect with the candidate or the ability to ask questions that you otherwise would not have thought to ask.

TOP TIP

Most candidates will have a LinkedIn profile – a great place to gather some quick insights to help develop the conversation.

The first thing to look at is whether you have a connection in common, which is a great conversation starter and will put the candidate at ease. For example, 'I've seen on your LinkedIn profile that you're a connection of (name) – I know them too. How is it you know them?' It also shows the candidate you have considered their profile and this is important as you have taken a bit of time to look at them by going outside their CV.

Next, look at the activity feed – this is where you can see all the latest bits of engagement the candidate has had with other people and things they have posted about that you may be able to ask about, for example, 'I saw your post on LinkedIn about (topic) that looked interesting, what made you decide to write about that?' At the bottom of the LinkedIn profile, you will also be able to see their interests in terms of businesses, technology or groups, a great place to get to know them on a deeper level and show you the types of things that make them tick. If you notice something here that you share a common interest in, it's another great rapport builder to factor into the conversation early on.

Outside LinkedIn, other popular places to look at someone for a tech position are GitHub (www://github.com) and Stack Overflow (www://stackoverflow.com). Just bear in mind that projects here can be old so are not always a true reflection of someone's current skills. It may be useful as a conversation piece, for example, 'I saw your project on GitHub/your answer on Stack Overflow – can you tell me a bit more about it?' Most tech candidates either blog or have their own personal websites. Again, this is a great place to scan and look for conversation pieces to build into the interview.

As a hiring manager, you will likely be asking questions within an interview. Ideally, this is to see how much research a candidate has done about you and your business. If you can tell they are well prepared, it's likely you will be impressed by the effort they have put in and get the feeling the candidate is super-interested in the position. The candidate will reciprocate this feeling if you do the same amount of preparation for them. The better you can make them feel about themselves, the more likely you are to see the real person open up and engage with you throughout the interview or conversation.

You will need to inform your recruiter of how the candidate needs to prepare. If you are only going to be talking about tech or if you are going to analyse an algorithm or do some scenario-based questions, be fair and give them the heads-up. I appreciate you will not want to provide the candidate with a full rundown of what to expect so that you can test their ability to think on their feet but grilling them on a specific technology in the first interview with no heads-up is unfair. The best thing to do is give a brief outline of what the specifics of the conversation will be. As mentioned earlier, the amount of preparation they do with the guidelines given to them will be a good opportunity to gauge how interested or motivated they are for the position. If you ask a candidate the simple question, 'What do you know about our business?' and they cannot answer, that's obviously a big red flag.

Regular updates

Having regular updates throughout a process is vital to ensure both you and the tech recruiter know precisely where you each stand and what is happening behind the scenes. There is nothing more frustrating than not knowing what is going on, or if you are not utilising your external recruiter fully. You need regular updates throughout the whole recruitment process to make sure you are not falling into this trap and are maximising your working relationship.

When working with a tech recruiter you may not see any progress initially, leaving you questioning whether they are trying to find candidates or working on the position. While it's great to receive candidates from your tech recruiter quickly, you should not always expect this. With specific requirements, it takes time to go through profiles, interview candidates, assess motivations and skill levels, and so on, in order to generate the strongest shortlist. A good recruiter takes this burden of time away from you, which is why you may not see anything for a week or two while this process is under way. Rest assured, however, that your tech recruiter will be working away. Here's a brief overview of what the search entails. The tech recruiter will most likely start with breaking the search down into two large lists to go through.

- **List one** will be from possible advert responses. Typically, most responses depend on where they are listed, but for example, one job advert in LinkedIn can receive hundreds of applications. I have found in my ten plus years in tech recruitment that 95% of those applications will not be suitable for the job, but as you can imagine, it takes a long time to go through them.

- **List two** will be from potential candidates the tech recruiter is trying to headhunt for the business – a much more suitable list of candidates but one that requires much more time as they will have to reach out to each person individually.

What you want to be wary of here is that your recruiter is not spamming people – a trap many poor recruiters fall into. A good recruiter knows that this part of the process takes time and approaching people in a personable and professional way is the best way to get results and to build up a good list.

From here, they must arrange calls and speak with each candidate individually to see if they are suitable, again taking a substantial amount of time.

A quick way to get an overview of what is happening is to agree on either a weekly or bi-weekly update on the progress, not the results. Ask your recruiter to send a short report on what they have done in the search so far. The key bits of information to ask them to include are:

- How many people have applied to the position?

- How many candidates have been prospected?

- How many conversations/interviews have been completed?

I also suggest asking the recruiter to make a note of all the reasons people decided to reject or not move forward with the position so that you can gather some data and business intelligence on what's causing people to drop off. This can help you identify any issues early on or to consider changing elements of your recruiting process to help attract more people in the future.

A common frustration from an external tech recruiter's side is not knowing where you are with the open position internally. Most recruiters know you are likely to receive applications from multiple sources and not just them. If you value working with your tech recruiter, you will want to make sure you are maximising the time they are spending on your account. Keep them informed of where you are with your position so that your recruiter knows whether to keep finding candidates, as well as keeping them motivated and interested in continuing to help you. Be transparent and open. You want your recruiter to feel like an extended arm of your business. The simple way to do this is to reply to your recruiter's weekly or bi-weekly update and give them a snapshot of your pipeline internally. This is especially useful if you are working on more than one position together. I recommend providing an overview of how many first, second, and final interviews you've had, and if you have an offer out, how likely you feel it is to close. This way the recruiter knows how much time to invest in your vacancy or whether it's worth focusing on alternative positions you might have open.

Interview feedback – the six pillars

After each interview, it is crucial to do a feedback round so that both you and the candidate can decide if it's worth moving forward. The best way to make sure you get the most out of feedback is to follow a structure called 'the pillars'. Each section is put in place to dig into the more profound thoughts of the candidate. The goal here is not just to hear positive feedback (which is good to know, of course), it's also to uncover any concerns or potential concerns so that you, as the hiring manager, can address these points in the following interviews (assuming that you would like to move forward with the candidate).

There are six pillars to consider:

1. Personal

2. Company

3. Role and responsibilities

4. Technologies

5. Concerns

6. Competition

Let's take a look at each pillar to see why they are important and what types of questions help uncover the answers you will need.

Personal

Personal is quite simply the connection the candidate has to you as the interviewer or hiring manager. As 'team fit' and personality play such a significant factor in deciding on whether or not to take a job, what the candidate thinks about you and whether your interview style has been well received is a good piece of feedback to understand. If you receive negative comments, do not take them personally but listen to what people are saying and try to adjust your interview technique accordingly. Do you jump into asking technical questions too quickly? Do you allow enough time for the candidates to ask their questions? Do you show no emotion during the interview? These are all things you can think about in further discussions to help better your process. Some open items I'd suggest your recruiter asks here are:

- How did you get on with the interviewer?

- How did the person interviewing you respond to your answers?

- How well did the interviewer explain the opportunity to you?

Company

Some companies are easy to understand, and it's obvious even before an interview what the company does, how it operates, how it makes money, what the vision, strategy and goals are, but for some it isn't. In this feedback pillar you want to get an understanding of what the candidates think and know about the company so far. Most candidates will want to understand whether or not they align with what the company does, how the vacancy fits into the business, how successful the company is, and how stable the business is. Here are some sample questions you will want your recruiter to ask the candidate:

- What did you find most interesting about this company?

- How does this company compare to your current company?

- What do you understand about the company so far?

- Is there anything about the company you don't like?

Role and responsibilities

As I referenced earlier, it still amazes me how many candidates have no further understanding of precisely what the role is and what the key responsibilities are after the first interview, apart from what they have read in the job specification. A candidate will want to understand whether they can identify with the challenges your job offers, whether they feel they can do the job justice, and what might be interesting about it. *You* will want to understand what the candidate thinks about the position. This way if any concerns come up, you can make sure you try to cover them in follow-on interviews, assuming both you and the candidate would like to continue with the recruitment process. Here are some excellent questions your recruiter should be asking:

- How do you think your skill set would fit this role?

- What do you find most challenging about this job?

- How well do you feel you fit this position and why?

- Based on what you know now about the role and the company, do you think this is the right position for you?

- Is there any part of the job you do not feel confident about?

Technologies

With any tech job, the tech stack that your company uses will often play a pivotal role in the candidate's decision. They will want to understand if the technologies you are using are ones that they are comfortable with and whether they will be able to develop their skill set. In the feedback, it's essential to know how strong the candidate feels they are at the core technologies you are using and if they believe they can do the job well. Typical questions your recruiter should ask are:

- What were your thoughts on the tech stack?

- How confident do you feel working on this tech stack and why?

- Are there any technologies they are using that you are not sure about using?

- Are there any processes or technologies that you're not familiar with? How would you approach developing your skills in these areas?

Concerns

Once you have discussed the opportunities that the new role provides, you will want to understand any concerns your candidate may have. Many people shy away from probing into this area as they don't want to hear any problems but it's so important. If you decide to ignore this part, even the smallest concern can grow and turn into a showstopper for a candidate if you do not face it head-on and try to solve it. The job of your recruiter is to understand what those concerns are. The benefit of working through a recruiter is that a candidate can feel more comfortable about voicing concerns here without the fear of upsetting or damaging their chances of securing the position. Even when a recruiter asks a candidate, they may still find it hard to voice any doubts. Some questions that can assist your recruiter to uncover concerns are:

- Is there anything about this opportunity you are unsure about?

- Would anything prevent you from moving forward with this position?

- If you were to score this position out of ten in terms of suitability, what rating would you give it?

- Is there anything that's missing that would make this the perfect opportunity for you?

Competition

With the demand for tech professionals rising, it's likely that the candidate you are considering is speaking with at least two other organisations. Again, your recruiter plays a vital role here to uncover who your competition is and where they might be in their process compared to yours, helping you to understand what you are up against and whether you need to expedite the process. What you need to remember is that the candidate's current employer is also your competition. No company likes to lose a good employee and finding a replacement takes a lot of time and money, so, as outlined earlier, it's becoming more common for candidates to receive counteroffers. Get your recruiter to ask:

- What other options do you have on the go at the moment?

- If any, where are you with those processes?

- How does this job compare?

- If your current employer asked you to stay, would you consider it?

- Under what conditions would you consider accepting a counteroffer?

Pre-empting counteroffers

As we know, the challenge for many businesses is the recruitment of highly skilled technical professionals for their open positions. On the flip side of this, companies also face the challenge of retaining their staff – the demand is high, and, in my experience, engineers are regularly contacted about new opportunities. I guarantee that when you make an offer to the candidate you want to hire they will receive a counteroffer from their current employer. The most frustrating part of the recruitment process is that you have done a lot of hard work to get to the point of making an offer which the candidate is happy with for it to then be taken away in one easy swoop by the candidate's existing company.

Why do companies make counteroffers?

Replacing staff with new employees is more expensive than retaining existing staff. The time it takes to find, interview and onboard new hires is widely underestimated, having a vacant position costs time and money, and the reduced productivity of the exiting employee is often overlooked.

Existing staff have specific skills and business understanding to carry out the job and for positions requiring niche skills in particular, it can be arduous to find and train new team members. Some industries have a candidate-led market due to a limited talent pool, so finding someone to hire with the relevant experience for the role in hand is even more difficult. Many employees, especially those in leadership roles, have a significant impact on the business, causing an increased loss of productivity across multiple employees if that leader leaves. A counteroffer can be a way to avoid this widespread cost to a business in the short term.

Here is an overview of what a company can expect to pay when filling a position:

- Agency recruitment fee – average of 10,000–15,000 EUR.

- Job adverts – between 500–5,000 EUR depending on where you place them.

- Hiring manager's time taken to make a new hire – based on my earlier example, an average hiring manager is paid 52 EUR an hour. An average process takes about six weeks. If they spend two hours a day for recruitment (writing job specifications, reviewing CVs, arranging interviews, conducting interviews, etc), that's 3,120 EUR without taxes and other insurances you pay on their salary.

- Time taken by team members to assist with interviews – based on an average salary of 60,000 EUR per member, this can range from 500–1,500 EUR.

- Person's leaving cost on team productivity and a skill shortage – this can range from anywhere between 1,000 to over 100,000 EUR depending on how critical your software/hardware or platform is.

- Notice period of one to three months – consider that your employee may be less productive in this time as they will ultimately have less motivation to complete tasks that they will no longer be a part of. For an average annual salary of 60,000 EUR, if their productivity drops, you will be effectively losing about 5,000 EUR a month, a total cost of 15,000 EUR.

- Onboarding time – this is the cost to the business while you allow for some time for the new employee to get up to speed. This can be anywhere from one to three months depending on the complexity of the job and skills of the new employee. Again, based on average annual salary of 60,000 EUR, the cost to the business is 5,000 EUR, potentially raising to 15,000 EUR.

Helping your candidate understand counteroffers

Although on the surface, a counteroffer may make an employee think that their company is finally pulling out the stops to make them feel appreciated, this is not usually the case. A counteroffer is not about the business reaching out to meet their needs, it's about meeting the needs of the company at that point in time. Counteroffers are frequently used as retention tools. This can be for a multitude of reasons – perhaps because a significant project is yet to come to fruition or because several other team members have recently departed, or in exceptional circumstances such as hiring freezes, a manager could simply be keen to retain them rather than have a gap in their department.

Counteroffers are often delivered alongside emotional leverage about their value to the team and the time spent there. Their existing manager may insinuate that the elusive promotion was in fact imminent, or that the team would struggle without their expertise. While many of these comments may be genuine, a good business that values its staff would have made them feel appreciated before they felt the push to leave.

It's not just about assessing the potential pitfalls of a counteroffer, but about considering the importance of new possibilities. Will staying at their current company offer the same long-term personal career development as moving to a new job position? While the existing employer might have offered more money to stay, these small gains in the short term might not pay off in the long run. It's also worth informing the candidate that between 70–80% of people who accept counteroffers either leave or are let go within a year,[7] so while

---

7 DigiTech, 'Should You Really Accept That Counter Offer?', nd, www.digitechsearch.com/job-coach/should-you-really-accept-that -counter-offer_1.htm, accessed 17 October 2020

accepting a counteroffer may seem beneficial initially, ultimately, they may be better off moving on to a new opportunity.

Coaching your candidate in counteroffers

When you speak to the candidate near the end of the recruitment process you will want to coach them on what's going to happen next as follows: 'When you accept a new job offer and hand in your notice, it's possible that your current employer will make a counteroffer to incentivise you to stay, typically in the form of an increased salary and benefits package, a promotion or a new and exciting project to work on.' I suggest including the following information for them to consider before they hand in their notice.

Seven reasons for not accepting counteroffers:

1. Broken trust: Your employer is now aware that you are unhappy so your commitment will be in question.
2. 'The grass isn't greener on the other side...': A phrase I hear all the time, but sometimes it is. You have taken the time to select the company you are going to carefully; you have met the new team and done your due diligence to ensure the new job will fulfil your goals.
3. Accepting a counteroffer rarely changes the factors that drove you to look for a new job in the first place, it merely papers over the cracks.

4. Where is the money for the counteroffer coming from – is it just your pay rise come early?

5. Statistics show that if you accept a counteroffer, there is a 70–80% chance you will be out of the job within a year.

6. Why do you have to threaten to resign before they'll consider giving you what you're worth?

7. What are their motivations for paying it to you now?

Ideally, your goal here is to get the candidate already thinking about this and testing their commitment to you and your job. What you want to hear is, 'Nope, there is nothing my current company can do financially or position/project-wise to keep me here, my mind is made up.' It is so important for the candidate to have made that mental agreement in their head at this part of the process as it's tough to break a promise to yourself.

In summary, you should expect that every candidate you decide to offer to will receive a counteroffer and with this information in your toolkit you should be able to convince the majority of your candidates to not even consider it. However, it's possible that you can go into a tug-of-war with the candidate's current employer and that you might have to be adaptable in your offer. Your recruiter can step in here to get valuable details to see what you can do to trump the situation and ensure you secure the person you want.

Making an offer

Making an offer should be by far the most exciting part of the process but it is often one that can be overlooked by many companies. At this point the candidate should be thrilled about the prospect of joining the business and you want to enhance this feeling, not become part of the process that lets you down. This section focuses on the time, delivery and impact that your offer should have so that when done correctly, the candidate is ready to commit straight away.

As an overview, this is what should be done to make sure you get that acceptance from the candidate:

- Discuss the offer you would like to make with your recruiter first – do not go straight to the candidate. If you get this wrong, there will be little you can do to make it right, and first impressions count. Make sure you are putting forward an offer that should *not* need any negotiation. Listen to your recruiter here. They should know whether or not what you are putting forward is going to be acceptable and what your chances are.

- Inform the candidate of the offer over the telephone and get their verbal commitment.

- Prepare your offer letter or draft contract. Have the majority of this prepared well in advance so that you only need to input numbers or personal details. I would highly recommend having a template. Most companies send something in black and white. While this is OK, I feel this is an opportunity to jazz things up, which I will come to later.

- Send the offer or draft contract to the candidate via email the *same* day you commit to making the offer. Do not lose any time here. Do not consider sending it by post – that's so 1990s and leaves you open for other companies to swoop in if you do.

- Put a time limit on the offer. You don't want to pressurise the candidate into making a decision, but you don't want to allow too much time in between either. Taking too long over a decision will often kill the deal and again, enable other companies to swoop in with their offer.

The period between making the decision and sending out the offer should be no longer than one working day. Anything more extended than that and I would start questioning why. Make sure your HR department knows something like this is a priority and a same-day task.

The delivery of the offer is an excellent chance for you to blow the socks off the candidate and make a lasting positive impression of what you and your company are all about. One of the best things I've seen in my time in recruitment was a company thoroughly preparing a PDF offer document of a few pages. They described in detail the offer, benefits, relocation guidance (where necessary) and the onboarding process and provided an internal point of contact and their external recruiter for additional questions. They also gave details on the current state of the business, including a clear overview of the vision, mission and expectations of the company. They gave a succinct outline of the expectations of the candidate within the business alongside short bios of the people in the team they would be working with. They even invited the candidate to one of their social events before they were due to start within the business. All of this was put into a visually appealing booklet.

So many businesses spend so much time on their website making their career page look awesome but fail to do the same when it comes to sending candidates they want to hire all the offer details. Most candidates won't revisit this page after applying and even forget some of the things you have tried to highlight as benefits. You may argue that if you have already done it on your website then you should not need to duplicate it, but if you can build a template that is customisable to each person you hire it will make them feel so wanted that it will be tough to turn down (assuming you have hit the right financials of the offer for them). After all, are you not trying to inspire your prospective new employee to think, 'Wow, they've done all this just for me, they must really want me there?'

Create urgency around your offer. While you of course want the candidate to have a reasonable amount of time to consider it, you also want them to accept it. Giving a shorter time frame prevents them from overthinking the offer and perhaps talking themselves out of it. I suggest time boxing the offer to one week, after which it is no longer valid. This is often referred to as an 'exploding offer'. Even if it's a candidate you want, you have to be prepared to walk away if they are unable to commit during this time. I would seriously doubt their commitment to joining you if they can't commit within the specified time frame.

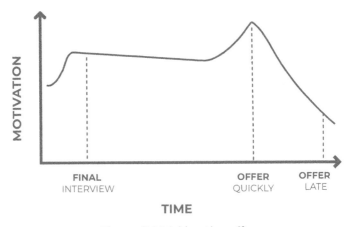

Figure 5.1 Making the offer

This is (probably) the first time this candidate has been offered a job with your company. Even if you have made a job offer a thousand times before, make sure each time is just as good as the first time you did – it will help cap off a remarkable recruitment process.

And remember, even if you don't end up hiring the candidate, having a process that is remembered for all the right reasons could lead to an application again in the future or referrals to other people.

SIX

Extra Care And Added Value

This chapter looks at extra things your recruiter or agency can do to add value to your company and provide you with the best recruitment service on offer.

Updates

The most critical information a recruiter can help you with is to know where you are with each opening. A reliable ATS to keep you up to date with the latest information specific to each candidate is invaluable. Your recruiter will have invaluable experience of using one of these. It helps keep you and the recruiter informed of what's going on and where to prioritise recruitment, particularly helpful when trying to recruit for multiple roles and when you are running several interview processes in parallel.

I recommend putting the most critical positions at the top, followed by the number of jobs for that role still open in a weekly or bi-weekly report. This helps give a picture of what your 'pipeline' looks like, including the people who have been approached, those who have been shortlisted and gone on to become candidates, and what interview stage your candidates are at.

For example:

Position	No. Open	CVs	1st Interviews	2nd interviews	Offers
Java Developer	2	4	3	1	1
FE Developer	1	2	1	0	0

Remember – updates are two-way. While your recruiter will be proficient at overseeing the ATS, the system can only remain relevant if you feed through the latest information to your recruiter. You can add to comments tied to each position. For example, adding notes can really help to keep the process running smoothly, such as 'Please stop recruiting for the Java role. We should close it soon if we secure the position from the people we already have in the process.'

When your recruiter has the latest information, they can then target where to spend their time. This allows them to maximise their recruitment focus for you so that you are covering as many of your openings as possible.

Your recruiter is then able to provide you with regular updates such as:

- How many people they have spoken to for each position

- How many CVs they have analysed

- What the market is saying about the position/s

- Whether the skills in question are possible to find or if there needs to be a trade-off for something else

- Whether there any areas in the company profile or job spec putting people off applying for this position

By doing this, you encourage a relationship with your recruiter which is open and transparent so you can work together to get the right people for your position and maximise your recruiter's time and motivation to find you the best tech talent there is. This tried and tested approach leads to increased productivity in recruitment, and a much a faster turnaround in filling the open vacancies.

Onboarding

When all the hard work from establishing a solid working relationship with an agency to closing a deal on a candidate is done, it's easy to think that the process is complete. Don't fall into this most deadly of traps. Most candidates typically have a notice period in their current position, which can usually be anything from one to three months. During this time, you want the candidate to feel connected to your business and not left to feel forgotten about until the start date. Onboarding is so much more than what you do with the candidate on their first day or first few weeks in a new job.

Ultimately, onboarding is the process of getting a new hire adjusted to your business quickly and smoothly where the candidate will learn the environment, culture and skill set needed to be able to function effectively. An excellent onboarding process can be vital to the candidate feeling welcomed into the company and be the difference between good and bad retention rates.

Your recruiter can be your secret weapon here. Ask them to keep in regular contact with your candidate to make sure everything runs smoothly from the point of signing the contract to the start date. They can act as an impartial point of contact should there be any questions during this transition period.

A recruitment agency worth their salt will be able to advise you on top working practices to make the onboarding process a success. Being well prepared is vital – as is considering the transition period from the new employee's point of view.

You should by now have a rough start date which you have agreed together. Where possible, offer some flexibility with proposed start dates to be able to respect your new employee's notice period and any other project or personal commitments they have. Once finalised, share the details with your team so they can also prepare to welcome their new colleague. A nice touch here is to encourage your team to connect with the new individual on LinkedIn before they start. This will really help them to establish a sense of belonging to the group and help build relationships before commencing work.

Start preparing things internally: collate all the documents and policies you need your new employee to sign on their first day. Make sure you have completed all necessary online accounts for them, along with the tech they need to be able to complete their work. It can be frustrating if the workstation isn't set up or equipment is missing and can leave a negative impression and a feeling of being undervalued. If you are hiring a tech person, it is always good to ask them what tech they are used to using, and where possible, accommodate them. It is becoming common for businesses to give candidates the choice of tech they want to use and tailor equipment to them, which is a nice touch.

A countdown to the start date

A few weeks before the start date, send out an onboarding form where you ask your new employee a variety of more targeted questions. You might like to include items on things like food preferences, allergies, favourite drinks, etc. You can then create a personalised welcome package. The less generic you can be, the more valued and welcome they will feel.

A few days before the start date, the best way to get a team member integrated is to take them out to lunch to help connect on a personal level. Plan this with the team to make sure as many of them as possible can attend. If you have an HR department, schedule in an onboarding meeting to go through all the documents and policies. Send the candidate a welcome mail informing them of what to expect and what their first tasks are likely to be, how to get to the offices, car park instructions (if needed), where to go and whom to ask for/meet first (this should ideally be the hiring manager or someone from the team they will be working with).

The day before the start date, run through your onboarding checklist and make sure all tasks are completed. Get the desk ready for the new arrival, including all paperwork, tech (make sure all is working), internal tools and online platforms with access codes, stationery, and your welcome package along with a welcome letter (ideally handwritten to create a more personal welcome). If you have a larger office, give them an office map as well as an organisation chart, upcoming special dates to be aware of, and any other reading material that is specific to your business or culture.

Welcoming your new recruit

On your new recruit's first day make sure you as the hiring manager can greet them, or if not, make sure it is someone from the team. Before sitting down, grab a drink together and give them a detailed tour of the office, introducing them to as many key people in the business as possible, leaving the direct team till last. From here, invite the new employee to an introductory meeting where you can outline the roles of everyone in the team, their function and what expectations you have as well as signing any necessary paperwork. Perhaps head out for lunch with the team, if possible, to get them integrated. Once back in the office, have them meet with HR to go through all the company's policies, then allow some time for them to login to all the necessary equipment and tools as well as kicking off any training or first tasks to complete.

During the first week, schedule any meetings or particular training days and set out some clear goals and performance-related objectives for the first few months. It's good to set out a road map for three-, six- and nine-month intervals on the projects the employee will be working on and provide regular feedback so that they know they are going in the right direction concerning tasks and performance. If the company is reasonably large, organise some meetings with other departments so that the employee can understand the different parts of the business and how they all work together. Be available for questions if needed. Continue regular one-on-ones throughout the next few months and be prepared to ask for honest feedback of what they think. Get their opinion on anything you might be able to improve on for future hires. You could even encourage them to write a company blog post (if you have one) of their experience of joining the business that you can later use in marketing material.

Following this onboarding process will help you welcome new people and help them to feel fully settled in their position, which leads to higher retention rates.

Stand out: Quick tips

In a world full of opportunities and where the demand is fully outstripping the supply for tech talent, it can be a real struggle to cut through the noise and stand out. In this quick-fire section I give you some ideas that you can either develop independently or with your recruitment agency to recruit the best tech talent you can by standing out.

- It's tough to compete with some large corporations on salary, but you can win on other advantages which are not just financially based. For example, you can highlight your culture, ethos and mission, maybe your tech stack, professional growth options, what's cool about the product you are building, or problem you are solving, and the people you are working alongside. Get all of these great things out on social media. Be prepared to make some engaging content, wherever you decide to post it, to pique the interests of passive candidates. I recommend a video as a great option to get your message out.

- Tech engineers have lots of organisations competing for their attention, but I've found that what drives a lot of them to consider something new are *technical challenges*. Be bold in your statement about the tech and projects you are working on and be prepared to give some specific examples in your job descriptions. Ask your current team what's sexy about this position from an engineer's point of view and create a smart, short statement to capture the attention of new talent.

- Attend meet-ups or events specific to your industry or technical area. Get involved where possible. Speak there or sponsor an event or attend with some swag from your company to promote your brand. The cost of doing so is relatively low compared to the reward you can gain. Think about how you are branding yourself and what you want people to know about your business and what it stands for.

- Be personable in your approach and do your homework on the candidate so you can include something in your opening line that relates specifically to their profile or that you found particularly interesting.

- Mix up your approach in how you target the business talent you're after. Ditch the emails you usually send and combine them with a video message instead. You will stand out over 95% of the competition and increase your likelihood of getting a reply from the people you want.

- Promise feedback and stick to it. It can be challenging to send everyone feedback, but if you invite a candidate to start an interview process with you remember they are taking a big step in considering a significant life decision and investing their time in this process. The least you can do if they are unsuccessful is to offer them some constructive feedback. Keep it short and simple but don't give your brand a bad rep by never going back to someone. You'd be surprised how many companies fall into this trap. Providing feedback will help you stand out and keep your reputation high even if you don't hire someone.

Creating a partnership

When working with an agency, it's easy to work together in a transactional way, which in most cases works OK. What this book should do is open your mind to how much more valuable a relationship with your recruiter or agency can be by creating more of a partnership. If you look closely enough, you may also be able to expand your network and develop this partnership to be even more useful for your business. Building a successful business is a team sport, and remember you have players in more places than you think.

As with most recruitment agencies, your agency is likely to have more than one customer. If they are a specialist recruiter, they are likely to be connected with other businesses that are similar to yours. Could your recruiter be the link to another company that could form a partnership with yours to take it to the next level? Think about that for a second. If you leverage a great relationship with your recruiter, have you ever thought about how their network (which is likely to be much larger than yours) could introduce you to previously unreachable people?

Of course, if you are in the technical area as a hiring manager it might not cross your mind but what if you were to speak to your sales and marketing team to see what other clients your recruitment agency has? I'm sure there will be some businesses in there that your company would like to get connected to and it's only one introductory call away. For example, I was working with a fantastic start-up that had grown reasonably well and was looking for investment. Due to the partnership I had with them, I was able to put them in touch with a venture capital (VC) business. The VC had funded another one of our customers and was one I felt would align perfectly with what they were looking for. Following an introduction, a substantial investment enabled the company to grow beyond what they thought was possible. I did not take a fee from this, nor did I expect to, I was just happy to support another one of my customers with what they needed as we had formed a great partnership. Just because your recruitment agency is tasked with finding suitable people for your business, your thinking should not stop there.

Suppose your company has a product that is B2B. Have you ever thought about the businesses your agency is connected with that could help catapult your sales? If you are connected, you are only one call away from making that happen. That's it. One call to your recruiter to make an introduction to one of their other existing customers could get you a meeting to pitch your business proposition to an otherwise unreachable person. I guarantee you – your recruiter will be glad to make that introduction. If it leads to a successful partnership, they will feel even more connected to your business and your success. Most agencies are proud to list who they work with on their website, especially if they are a well-known, global brand. If not, it's always worth-while having that conversation with your recruiter. Take a look or have that conversation with them to see what else you can gain from your existing partnership to create new and fruitful ones.

There are partnerships everywhere. Being connected to a successful agency is a natural link to some great opportunities for your business if you know where to look or how to ask for them.

Conclusion

Thanks for taking the time to read *Remarkable Tech Talent*. It should provide you with the architecture to be successful in attracting and retaining A-player candidates. Some of the principles in this book can also be applied to any type of recruitment within your business. Recruitment is no longer just another task in a business's life cycle – it has become one of its most critical parts. It's the foundation of people who make your business successful and that all starts with your recruitment and how you approach it.

You should now be clear on how to set up your internal recruitment process as well as your partnership with your recruiter; have clearer goals and objectives; and have the knowledge to ensure they are representing you in the best way possible. The strategies and tips shared will result in a more streamlined process to attract the most qualified candidates with the least fuss.

I hope you have found this book useful. If you implement just one part of what I've shared with you, I hope it helps your business to have a fantastic recruitment process and secure more of the people you want.

I wish you all the best in making your recruitment remarkable.

Acknowledgements

I truly am blessed with so many excellent people in my life – friends and family and those I've met during my career, including mentors, supporters, partners, clients, candidates – each of whom has played a role shaping me into the man I am today. They have helped me learn a lot along the way to get to the point of writing this book.

A special acknowledgement to Daniel Priestley from DENT and Lucy McCarraher from Rethink Press who first planted the seed in my mind that this is something that I should do. Without them, this would not be possible and probably would not have happened.

Thanks to my business partners Chris Proctor and Claire Jones, my robust support network who give me inspiration and energy every day and make running our business a real delight.

Thanks to my family for always being there for me, especially in times where things got tough and I wondered how I would get by every month. Mum, you are incredible at knowing the right things to say and to spur me on in those times. I'm forever in your debt and always want to make you, Dad, Claire and Sarah proud of me.

Thanks to my team of 'DigiTekkers' at DigiTech Search who continue to do a fantastic job at supporting our clients and candidates by following these methods and who gave me space and time away from the day-to-day business needed to write this book.

I'd also like to thank Paul Kirby and Daniel Mulholland who gave me my first break into technical recruitment and who both taught me a lot. My start in this area could not have been any better and I couldn't have done it without your support. I often look back at those times working for you with a smile on my face, with great memories of our 'work hard, play hard' attitude.

Thomas Ludwig, you gave me inspiration and ability to start my business, and after so many years of working together, I don't think you entirely realise the impact you have had on my life. I want you to know I am truly grateful for everything you have done for me and look forward to working with you for many years to come.

To my wonderful peer group – Jonathan Hemus, Andrew Armitage, Sophie Milliken and Simon Shepard, who have been continuously pushing me to complete this book as well as advising me on so many other things. Thank you.

Michael Maretzke, reading and re-reading this book, giving me some valuable insights and direction. Generously offering his time and being so supportive. Thank you.

For my beautiful daughter Elouise, who I hope one day will read this and be proud of me and see it as proof that you can do anything you set your mind to.

The Author

Paul Turner is a technical/IT headhunter and co-founder of DigiTech Search, which he runs with his sister Claire Jones and his life-long friend Chris Proctor. Their specialist technical recruitment business supports businesses throughout Europe but mainly within UK, Germany, Austria, Switzerland, Netherlands, Sweden, Norway, Denmark, Finland and Iceland, and was a 'new business of the year' finalist in the 2019 Business Excellence Awards.

Paul has over a decade of experience in scaling and powering up the digital capabilities of tech teams across Europe and a strong track record, having placed over a thousand full-time professionals into key positions for businesses such as Nokia (now HERE maps),

1&1 Internet/GMX, Zalando, Groupon, Mesosphere (now D2iQ) and PayPal. He has helped some start-up businesses catapult into unicorn status by securing exceptional talent during scale-up stages, giving companies the platform of people to achieve greatness.

He started off in recruitment as a junior and worked his way up through progressive leadership positions so when it comes to tech recruitment he's been around the block and knows a thing or two about how things should be done and what it takes to make the recruitment process and partnership exceptional. He is passionate about raising funds for charity and works primarily with B1G1 to support the UN's global goals for sustainable development, and the Raspberry Pi Foundation which helps young and underprivileged children to code.

For further information or insights or if you would like to take a test to see how your current recruitment process stacks up, visit https://digitech.scoreapp.com for a free, detailed report and some more useful advice.

Paul is available on most social media platforms, particularly the ones below. Feel free to visit these for more insights or if you would like to get in touch.

- 🌐 www.digitechsearch.com
- 💼 www.linkedin.com/in/paul-turner-6720a8136
- 🅱 www.digitechsearch.com/digitech-community /blog
- ▶ DigiTech Search

Lightning Source UK Ltd.
Milton Keynes UK
UKHW020723030221
378158UK00006B/180